Brain Power Strategies

How to Avoid Distraction and Keep Your Concentration

(Proven Memory Hacks Tricks and Strategies for Improving Your Memory)

James Hager

Published By **Andrew Zen**

James Hager

Brain Power Strategies: How to Avoid Distraction and Keep Your Concentration (Proven Memory Hacks Tricks and Strategies for Improving Your Memory)

ISBN   978-1-998769-11-7

No part of this guidebook shall be reproduced in any form without permission in writing from the publisher except in the case of brief quotations embodied in critical articles or reviews.

Legal & Disclaimer

TABLE OF CONTENTS

Chapter 1: Experiencing The Mind's Power

Swami Vivekananda in his own words, has stated...

"Mind powers are like sunlight's rays. If they are focused, they illuminate."

The Mind as a Energy Source

It is believed that the Mind Over Matter theory is not a myth that has been disproved. Through the years the science has proven the power of our thoughts over our bodies. in the event that we manage them, they can control the body's as well. Thoughts can have physical manifestations that affect our behaviours and behavior.

One of the most significant discoveries made by scientists regarding this theory is the Placebo drug that is a fake drug that is safe and is essentially made from sugar. It is designed to convince the patient that they are using medication to treat their illness.

The drug has been effective in treating anxiety and depression as well as other physical ailments, decreasing symptoms and stress. It is just the notion of these patients were taking medication to heal their ailments, resulted in their brains anticipating the success effects of these medications that resulted in their bodies responding to a degree that it resembled health. Utilizing PET scanners, and MRIs scientists took the next step in explaining how the brain operates in conjunction with the placebo. When a dummy drug is administered, the brain of the patient alters the chemical balance in the brain, causing it to alter its physical responses and also. The chemical changes are translated into body-wide responses itself.

This discovery offers us an idea that the brain is capable of performing things that go beyond our expectations.

The Power of Concentration in the Mind

One of the most important features and goals of life is the ability to perform tasks effectively and efficiently. To accomplish this task, it requires the use of a mind.

Maybe you've been completely absorbed in a book was on your shelf or watching a film you were watching that everything else was blurred into a background you weren't conscious of. Your brain was focused. It is the brain's capacity to focus or direct our attention to whatever it is we wish to do and to deviate from our focus whenever we wish to do so, and vice versa. Concentration is one of the brain's capabilities which can be assisted through the strength of our minds as well as the concept that the mind is superior to matter.

You may also thought about something else during the discussion or meeting. Maybe you've attempted to read a whole paragraph before you finally pondered what you just read. It occurs. Attention is a finite resource and concentrating can be quite challenge. A lot of times, we are prone to wander mindlessly around.

The area of our brain that is responsible for our ability to concentrate and be attentive is known as the prefrontal cortex lateral. The neurons within this region communicate with one another to filter out the information they receive from the surrounding environment using the sense of sight. They filter out distractions from the data, making concentration more efficient and effective.

We all have the capacity to concentrate at times, provided that we put our effort and energy to accomplish it. That means we aren't able to do it particularly with the numerous distractions in our lives. Mental concentration requires effort. Mental effort requires practice.

Our brains must practice strategies for concentration in order to concentrate properly. This complete improvement in the capacity to focus will not be accomplished within a flash of the eye neither will it be achieved in a single day. The brain needs to be exposed to these methods of concentration in order to focus effectively and efficiently, but it can take weeks or months. Therefore, you must be patient and never abandon the effort. Attention is a finite source initially however, with consistent effort and persistence it will become the most powerful source of power in completing many tasks with ease.

The months and weeks of work will not go in vain because you'll require a lot of concentration to do various things, from cooking, driving, to learning as well as working to a myriad of other things throughout our day-to-day lives. It can be applied for almost every aspect of our lives, so putting in the time and energy to mastering it isn't an unimportant thing to do.

It is only just a tiny portion of our brain each day, and we're not conscious of its total capacity and capabilities when it is used effectively. Mind power is among the most powerful and effective methods to help you accomplish things effectively. The power is mostly based on our thoughts. Being aware of the fact that they are our thoughts, gives us the ability to harness this ability effectively, if we pay attention and control of our thoughts. They shape and define our character and affect all things in our life. It is therefore a must capability focus and stay clear of distractions.

Benefits of Having Control Over Your Mind

Before you begin to implement the methods to maintain your focus and unwavering, consider what you will gain from these strategies. The benefits of power of the mind can be found in all areas of your life, from the most challenging task that you must complete all the way to the simplest one. The more control you have over your mind, the better you'll be able to focus and reap these advantages.

1. Clarity of Thoughts

The ability to control over your thoughts and mind means that you can rid your mind of unnecessary or negative thought patterns. They will only cause you to be stressed and hinder you from completing important things. By removing these thoughts, you can bring peace of mind as well as a focus on your thoughts, which will make you think more clear.

2. Better Memory

Since you are able to clear your mind of unimportant thoughts, you will be more attentive to more relevant information. Being clear of these distractions allows your brain to take in the information more effectively, meaning that it will be retained for a longer period of time and even more effectively.

3. Higher Self-Confidence

The power of our mind allows us to focus on our own thoughts. But, with the right self-reflection we are able to look at ourselves as people with flaws, as well as positive characteristics. The more we are aware of these aspects, the more we recognize our own limitations. We increase our self-efficacy and increase the confidence we have for ourselves.

4. Efficient Comprehension

In the absence of any other thoughts that distract you It is easier to focus on the process of processing information. The more you pay attention an item, the faster you are able to process it swiftly and efficiently.

5. Happyness and improved mood

Another benefit of having the power to control your own thoughts is the ability to force a positive feeling on yourself. This helps you relax or decrease the level of stress hormones in your body, which is known as cortisol. When you can focus, your mind is in good shape to concentrate on more positive things, instead of dwelling on concerns and anxieties. You can relax and let go of the burden, which reduces the chance of developing depression.

6. Improved Emotional Regulation

Concentration can help you achieve an improved mental outlook and an attitude-driven emotional state. This is because you increase your ability and willpower to take on the world and overcome the challenges you face instead of absconding from them.

7. More Productivity

Concentrating on a particular task for an extended period of time will allow you to be more efficient. Concentration makes it less likely to move between tasks so which means you don't have an end product. Furthermore, since you can give 100% focus to the task at hand as well as giving importance to the quality and quality of the output, recognizing that your focus will not drag down the quality of the output. Concentration will enhance your performance, both in output and productivity quality.

8. More Neural Connections

Mind power doesn't only require evidence from behavior. It also goes to the neural level within the brain. Regular practice of concentration will help your brain build greater and more powerful connections that help make your processing faster. You are able to shift tasks simultaneously one task and still be attentive to the tasks at hand this is when your ability to concentrate has been developed already.

9. Enhanced Creativity Abilities

Concentration helps our minds develop innovative and imaginative concepts. By avoiding distractions, we can make your brain focus focused on what it's supposed to. If you're planning to make a design or art, it's best to be in the moment in order to get more of a sense of your work.

10. Safety and Security

If you're not paying attention to the things you're doing, the chances are that your mind may let crucial security precautions go unnoticed and you could end up in a crash. There have been many road accidents that were caused by multitasking when driving. The lack of focus can cause more damage than you can ever imagine. Think about your thoughts wandering when you iron your clothing. The more you wander and the more clothing gets burned. Concentrating on your work will help you avoid unintentional accidents that could result in harm.

Chapter 2: Enhancing Your Mind Power

Tilopa, Tibet said that Tilopa, Tibet said that...

"In first, the person who meditates is able to feel as though his mind is falling like a stream that falls through the ravine. Then it slows down like the gentle meandering River Ganges And finally the river is one with the vast Ocean and it becomes one with the Lights of Son which is called the self, along with Mother or the base of being, become one."

If the advantages of the mind's power concentration are convincing, you may be wondering how your brain develops to its enthralling state.

The process of developing your mind's power is similar to enhancing the physical power. This requires lots of perseverance, patience and repetition. All of the efforts will pay off when your mental power is fully developed. This will make it simple for you to avoid distractions and focus on completing your goals.

According to the most classic of spiritual texts the power of your mind will go through three stages that encompass the capacity to be easily distracted as well as a gradual improvement on attention and becoming an individual with the goal of your concentration.

The growth process starts by being able hold your attention briefly on an activity. The distractions can take your attention from time to time some time, and finishing the task might take longer than when you focus your on it, paying attention to it, and putting your focus on it. At this point your focus will slowly become maintained. Even though it is initially moments of focus The more you are involved in it and the longer you engage in it, the stronger it becomes. For instance, if you are able to focus on something for seven breaths, then the next thing is that you're engaged in a project for 21 consecutive breaths as long as 108 breaths or more, without losing focus. This is the improvement.

The second phase is when your focus can be sufficient stable to not lose focus, even when there are periodic distractions and temptations that come. You build a stronger relationship with the subject of your attention that your brain doesn't drift away from it as quickly. At this point you will feel feelings of being connected and a sense of fluidity between you and the subject of your attention.

In the third phase the mind becomes so strong that it can go beyond the feeling of being connected, but also the connection between you and the subject of your concentration. It is the time when your mind is so absorbed by the subject or task in concentration, and engages in a unified effort with the subject and totally eliminates all distractions. At this point, more than just removing any distractions, you experience more connected to the task that makes your focus more focused.

If you have a well-developed concentration and focus, you'll be able to tap into your mental power for any job you are doing. Being able to stay focused isn't an easy task but, with patience and persistence, as well as practice accessing your mind's maximum potential isn't an unattainable goal.

Concentration Killers

The distractions or killers of concentration can be found in a variety of varieties and in different degrees from external or internal sources. They could be in your way or you may decide to remove them from your way to get your job done. Before you accomplish that, you must to get familiar with yourself with these killers of concentration to ensure that the next time you are confronted with them, you'll be able to think about how to avoid them , and quickly note that you need to steer to avoid them in a more effective manner. These are the most commonly used inhibitors of concentration that can prevent you from getting anything completed:

1. Multitasking

Multitasking can give you the impression that you're working on two or more tasks at the same however, in reality the only thing you're doing is shifting between tasks and then to another but not completing anything. Multitasking causes you to waste time as you shift between various tasks you don't actually do anything about, or even if you accomplish something it, the quality of the results of these tasks could be in danger. Multitasking can cause your attention to be divided as you switch from one job to the next. This doesn't work particularly when the tasks that are being completed are complex and urgent ones. It's okay to make calls while you draw, but it's an entirely different matter when you're cooking or doing your ironing. Multitasking is only feasible with simple tasks that you've already mastered well. However, other than this, it can be the leading cause of loss of concentration.

2. Absence of interest

If you aren't keen to complete something, nearly every thing can keep your attention from carrying out the task. Maybe you've tried to study for a class, but nothing interested you, and you find yourself staring at a wall more intriguing than reading your textbook. It is possible that boredom will take over all your concentration working on a project, which makes you more likely to give to distractions. The lack of enthusiasm could lead to a lack of taking action too. Therefore, if you realize that something isn't appealing to you enough, prepare yourself for a battle in completing the project.

3. Fear and the negative thoughts

Our thoughts have such power over us that if we're focused on them, they are able to control and prevent us to not pay attention to other issues. Perhaps you've had to worry about a test coming up or the impact of something you've have said, or even not having any money even. These thoughts can be so overwhelming which means that for the majority often it is the only thing we think about. They take up space in our brains that should be devoted to things more productively, but instead of focusing on more pressing issues our minds are at a loss and physically paralyzed.

4. Electronic Gadgets

Our phones ring and, like it's an automated response, we reach for the phone and respond immediately. We are distracted and keep them in close proximity. The constant stream of instant messages, text messages, and emails prompt us to feel the desire to respond whenever we get them . We stop time when we're busy to check these messages. When our attention is split between our work and the demands of these electronic devices that we can't concentrate fully on doing what's needed.

5. Internet

It can be a constant difficult task to access the internet while you're trying to complete a task. You might find yourself working on your own for five minutes, and then, before you know it you're browsing Facebook as well as Twitter for the next half hour or so. The ease of multitasking online can make it a risky location to fall prey to distracting activities.

6. Fatigue

Fatigue is our entire system's biggest adversary. If you're so exhausted that you feel you're floating around all day, just waiting to see the sun set you'll be unable to focus on things that aren't important. A lack of sleep can hinder the ability to focus, short-term memory as well as other mental functions.

7. The Side Effects of Drugs and other medical conditions

The inability to concentrate could also be caused by medical conditions, such as ADHD sleep apnea anemia, depression, or thyroid disease and more. It is recommended to talk with your physician or psychiatrist about these medical concerns when you begin to notice the signs.

8. Noise

Noisy environments divert your attention from things that aren't necessary. Instead of focusing on your work your brain is distracted by unnecessary and disturbing noises. Your attention is split so that you are unable to focus fully on the task in hand.

Chapter 3: The Distracted Mind

Thoughts can come into our minds whether or not we have conviction. If we don't exercise control of these thoughts, they could distract us and prevent us from thinking about other important things.

An unfocused mind can take up a lot of your time, which could have been devoted to productive tasks instead.

New research studies have demonstrated how the brain operates when it is focused or is distracted. It has been discovered that these two processes take place in distinct areas of the brain. The brain is focused on paying attention, while another area is activated when our senses are distracted.

The study was carried out using an experiment conducted with monkeys. Subjects were shown an attention-tester by way of a video screen in exchange for apple juice as a reward. They were asked to focus and select a specific object that they could focus their attention on, such as the red box leaning towards the left-hand edge of the screen.

But, flashes of attention-grabbing stimuli are observed during midway through the test. When monkeys were able to focus on particular parts that they were focusing on, the frontal region of their brain , which is known as the prefrontal cortex showed significant amounts of stimulation. When attention grabbers were seen in the brain, activity were highest in the back of the brain, also known as that of the parietal cortex.

We now know the way it works to focus and distract our brains, we can see how to deal with these issues. Furthermore, realizing that these processes operate independently of each other in terms of specific brain areas' activity and brain areas, we can increase possibilities of working with both independently, by improving concentration and decreasing distractibility.

Self-Regulation Strategies

Concentration is dependent on two of our main abilities: to eliminate and focus. Both of these skills can be achieved through a high degree of self-regulation. Concentration is the ability of the mind which allows us to direct our focus to something, and also to refocus our attention whenever we need and want to. However, with all the distractions and distractions all around us, we frequently struggle to focus all our focus on an individual task until we finish it. In many cases, we are thinking about something else while working, or scrolling through various social media websites for hours when we said we'd only get a 5-minute study break.

The process of telling ourselves to stop and work is much more challenging than we realize this is why it's important to master self-regulation methods in order to instruct ourselves when to begin working and stop putting off work.

If our self-control isn't in control, we are more susceptible to temptations and distractions. Our mood swings, cravings and impulses could cause us to lose our balance. The weakness of our self-control can cause poor concentration as we are unable to decide the things we should be focusing on. Untrained minds and actions that are impulsive are not the best combo for concentration. Learn these strategies for self-regulation to help you be able to direct your focus.

1. Get Here Now

If your mind begins to wander off in other directions, remember the following three phrases: "Be here now!" These words to prevent your mind from wandering away from your mission and get back in the right direction.

2. Learn from the Spider

If you let a tuning fork to make a sound on a web of spiders and the spider begins to search for the cause of the vibration. But, eventually the spider will realize that it's you having fun and not a bug waiting to take down the web. The spider then is back at work building its web in peace.

If spiders are able to do it and you can, then you should be able to too. Consider their weaving while accomplish your own work. The ability of spiders to switch their focus to what they're doing, and not be distracted is the same kind of concentration the brain capable of. If you're in the middle of your class or at work when someone comes in the space. It is possible to turn your head to look. However, if you're working on something important, then it is not necessary to look around and could end up being unproductive of your time. Make sure you don't allow yourself to be a victim of distractions. Instead, focus on what you must be doing. When someone comes into your room, you must train yourself to not look at them and keep working, learning from the spider's focus.

3. Be Worried Later

Schedule a time for you to be worried and reflect on all the thoughts that are making you feel anxious. Research has shown that having regular time to worry reduces the amount of worry you are putting on your mind by 35% over the course of 4 weeks. If you have a troubling idea outside of your regular worry time, simply brush it off with another self-regulation method (i.e."Be there today!) and remind yourself that you'll be able to deal with it in the future. Put off any worries that are distracting you until the time you have scheduled to worry.

Also, you should plan a specific time for your stress. It could be in the evening between 7:00 and 7:30 pm , or whatever time frame you prefer. Remember the clean anxieties you faced throughout the morning. It is likely that you will be able to forget about the concerns you were expected to consider at the moment. In other instances, you might also recall the worries. When you recall these thoughts, you'll be more clear and this means that your concerns could be able to be solved in the near future.

4. The hedge

Start by experiencing having a certain amount of inertia when working on a particular task. After about five minutes then, you can decide if you'd like to keep working or have time off. If you choose the latter option, ensure that you've got your kitchen timer set so that you can go right back to work following breaks. In this way, you'll be able to take a break and regain your focus and achieve your goals slowly.

5. Participate in a Rewards System

Who doesn't want to see their dividends? Who wouldn't like to celebrate something has been accomplished with success? Set yourself simple goals when you've completed your task. Make sure you are rewarding yourself according to the amount of effort you require or the effort you've worked to complete them. If you complete a difficult or important job then you might want to treat yourself to a nice meal, a film or an hour of web surfing, or something else that is more valuable to you. If your tasks are merely basic, you could take part in smaller rewards too. You can take the time to read five pages from a particular book that you've been wanting to get your hands on, or scroll through Facebook in 10 mins. Be sure that the goal and the reward is in line with each other, and can also be sure that it is in line with the effort you put into it. When rewarding yourself, it's important to remember that you're doing it to yourself and not for insufficient efforts .

6. Tally Lapses

While you're engaged in a particular task put aside a pen and a piece of paper and count the amount of times you've been distracted by things that are not related to your work. Keep track of the time spent distracted and also. This will allow you to keep track of the times you've strayed from the topic you thought was your focus. This will set off an alert if you've been slowing down far too much. It will also encourage you to return to work, stay focused and work harder.

One of the hardest people to control it's us. Sometimes , we get carried away and forget about we need to are reminded of.

Once you've achieved success in delegating work in deciding which tasks to concentrate on, you'll find it much easier to manage other elements of focus (such like the surrounding or your diet). In the majority of cases self-doubt is the most difficult to battle. But with hard work and determination, overcoming yourself is a satisfying and rewarding task that will be a great way to achieve greater and more effective results.

Strategies to Boost Concentration

Different types of concentration killers can be dealt with differently and in a specific way. If you are aware of the obstacles that you are facing as the aforementioned concentration killers when you are trying to accomplish tasks, here are some strategies to combat them in a direct manner:

Multitasking

1. Plan Your Work

If you are able to do a lot of tasks at once there is a chance that you do not know where to begin , so you have to do everything at once or do nothing whatsoever. If you plan everything you must complete within a given day, and set a the appropriate time allocated for each task, you'll be able to be aware of what tasks you must put your energy at a specific moment in the day. As an additional suggestion, you can schedule your most difficult and most demanding tasks for the morning, in the morning when your motivation is at its highest. You can follow these assignments with easier ones so all the other aspects of the day can be a breeze.

2. One step at a time

If you've already created your timetable, stick to it and complete one thing after another. The schedule you have created is not to complete the tasks in a unified manner, but to allow the time needed for each. Making each task distinct keeps you focussed on completing each of them.

3. Don't Get Lost in Distractions

Certain things can keep you from doing more than just one thing at a. Your smartphone could be a tool to keep you from accomplishing your work because you're always thinking about it. Keep your phone out of sight and switch off the television. Clean up your area to avoid picking up distracting objects.

Mental Thoughts

1. Let the thoughts come and go.

Your thoughts could be as waves that splash onto the shore. They can change just as they do. The way you look at them can cause you to think about other ideas and issues that weren't ever really present in the beginning. Try letting your thoughts flow and disappear. If you are beginning thinking about something allow it to come into your thoughts but don't provide any judgment or analysis. Just let the thought take place. When it is finished, as it cameto you, let it go. This might be difficult at first , but after a lot of practice, it will make it easier to stay away from worry and other negative thoughts.

2. Plan your Trip

Make a calendar of your daily and weekly schedules. One reason people get anxious is that they aren't sure what's coming up in the coming days. After you've laid out the tasks you need to complete within a month, the course of a week and the course of a day, you will know exactly where you're going. Make a plan and you will have control over what happens that take place in your life. So, you will be less worried about what's likely to happen because you know you're headed towards a destination.

Fatigue

1. Get Regular Exercise

One of the primary reasons you can't have a great quality sleep is due to a problem with your overall health and wellbeing. Involving in regular workouts and in combination with a healthy diet will help you get a better night's sleeping throughout the night.

2. Pause for a break

The body and your brain only function for a specific amount of time. In the absence of breaks between tasks the system can be unable to function properly in the long term. You should allow yourself a decent amount of time to relax between things. You should take a break. So when you next perform your task you'll be rejuvenated and, consequently more productive. If you're aware of the term "power nap', then you recognize its importance especially for retention.

3. Find Your "Prime Time"

There will come a point during the day that you'll be extremely productive, and you could call it the "prime period". Find out if your work is best during the day, later in the afternoon, or later in the evening, complete your work at your peak time, so that you don't end up making your body work all day long.

4. Be aware of your body

Your body is likely to display signs that indicate that it's not performing well, be aware of how you can listen to it. If you begin to feel sicker and more exhausted than normal and you are feeling tired, you may be able to take some time off. Be aware it is the capital of your working. Without it you won't be able to be at your best, therefore don't take your health for granted.

Insufficiency of Interest

1. Reconnect

One of the possible reasons for your loss of enthusiasm for completing a task is that you have lost its significance. When you reach a certain point in the course of your work you'll forget why you were doing it at all in the first place. All you need to do is revive your passion for your job. You can think about the reason you were enticed to take on it at all in the first place. It could be a subject you did not really like, however, you should ask yourself the reason you decided to enroll yourself in it. Perhaps it was because of the desire to finish. Keep your head up and keep doing it with the sake of a goal.

2. Be Active

There are jobs that do not keep you interested since they're plain boring. However you can add some spice through working at them regularly. If you're working on something that is boring You might want to be able to talk to yourself when studying , or use highlighters while writing notes or taking notes. It will make the work more enjoyable and interesting for yourself to allow you to focus on it for several long hours.

3. Work with a person

The majority of your time alone, and can become boring. Partnering with someone can bring a new dimension in whatever you're working on. If you have to concentrate on completing a piece of work in class, find a friend at a cafe and begin working on your essay. The added pressure will enhance the performance of your tasks which will make you more efficient. The majority of people work best when under stress.

Electronic Gadgets

1. Switch Off Your Gadgets

There is no need to keep ringing when you shut off your electronic devices. Put it away and put them away for a few minutes. You can concentrate on your task with the tab or phone in front of you. Switch it off and put it away from your view to stay clear of temptations. Test this out and see the changes.

2. Switch off Social Media Notifications on your phone or tablet

If shutting off your device could be too difficult for you, then at the very minimum, turn off social media notifications that make your phone ring once or twice. Knowing that someone has posted a comment on your post will prevent you from figuring out what the person commented on. Beware of the potential harm these gadgets could make you feel by turning off the notifications.

3. Don't work near the TV

The closer you are close to an electronic device the more vulnerable you are to it. As much as is possible when you're doing something important be sure to stay clear of electronic gadgets like televisions, particularly because it may captivate our attention very quickly and easily.

Internet

1. Choose to use Minimal Tabs

Use only the tabs essential to the job you're working on. Beware of logging into the social networks you use or other websites that can distract you from your work. Choose to use fewer tabs and achieve maximum efficiency.

2. Utilize the Utilities

The internet can also aid you in staying away from all the internet's distractions. Utilize different tools like Greasemonkey script that is available within Mozilla Firefox with Greasemonkey extension. You can make use of the invisibility Cloak as well as Kiwi Cloak to block, for a specific duration, websites that make you lose your focus. Additionally, you can make use of Time to Go. This allows you to connect to the sites that cause concentration loss for a specific period of time. Then, at least you will know precisely which sites you'll return to.

3. Switch off your Internet Connection

If you are unable to maintain your own, the best solution is to simply shut off Internet access and do your work offline. With no internet connection it is unlikely that you'll be enticed to sign in to any website.

4. Use a time-out to relax.

One reason why you are unable to work and fail to concentrate is the overload of focusing on a task at a specific time. when you next take a look you realize it's no longer making any sense. Relax and unwind for a bit. Take a break of five to 10 minutes. You could browse the various websites you thought distractions, but be sure that you're able to bring yourself back to a standstill at the point you realize you must return to work. And then, get back to work. After this your brain is rested and relaxed, and your brain can perform greater efficiency and effectiveness in processing. This allows you to concentrate better.

Noise

1. Silent Spot

Find a spot or hideout to work without much background noise. It could be in a café or your bedroom or in the library of your school. Find a comfortable place and get started working on your project and you'll succeed.

2. Create Your Own Music List

The way we perceive what sounds like could vary. Many prefer to work in a quiet background while others view music from rock as soft. Whatever your preference for music may be, you can pick your music and make your own studying or working playlist. Be sure to ensure that you do not spend the entire time singing along to the entire playlist instead.

Chapter 4: Exercises For Concentration

As with muscles, your brain power requires lots of repetition to develop its full capacity of concentration. The practice of this skill requires dedication and perseverance for it to grow fully. This is the reason you need to perform regular exercises of concentration. Within your routine you should set aside time to exercise your focus. You can try different exercises listed in this chapter.

Here are some examples to help keep your brains active and communicating, creating more efficient pathways to think. These exercises can help you get comfortable with doing tasks, rather than reacting to distractions constantly. It might be beneficial to try these techniques to fully experience the benefits of being able to increase your ability to focus to the fullest extent:

1. The Counting Backwards

Start counting backwards from 100. Focus your mind on your next numbers. If thoughts come up but they are not important, let them go and then pay attention to that next one. It is also possible to do an exercise similar to this using the method of counting backwards with threes. Start with 100, then 97, 94, and so further, etc., on. It is also possible to focus on counting backwards in fours or twos, or if would like, by prime or composite numbers too.

2. Word Focus

Choose a word that has inspired you. You could either say the word out loud or hold it in your mind. If you are distracted by other thoughts you, turn your attention to the word and speak it out loud, or repeat it in your head.

3. Fruit Focus

Pick any fruit you like and place it with one hand. Be aware of your fingers along the sides, feel the softness of the skin and smell the freshness. Pay attention to the qualities of the fruit. If you are distracted by thoughts then immediately shift your focus and back on the fruit. Try this for at least five minutes.

4. Whole Watch Way

Pick a random object that is near you, whether it's glass, a pen or a fork. Take a look at the object's shape as well as its color and edges without speaking about the things you've observed. Focus on the specifics and features of the objects. You might not realize there are parts of them you haven't actually noticed. Take at least five minutes doing this exercise.

5. Stay Still

Find a comfortable sitting position and get at ease. Concentrate your attention on your body being still and still. If you do move, shift back into concentrating immediately. Try this for five minutes at minimum. Do it in 10 or 15 minutes and maybe more if you are already able to. Challenge yourself.

6. Close-Open

Place yourself in a chair next to an area where you can place your hands on top of it. Relax your hands and extend out your hands away from table. Slowly, you can open your firsts, and then look towards your fingers as it slowly expands its fingers. Then, slowly open it and concentrate on the opening. You should not be thinking about anything aside from the stretching and opening of your fingers and palms.

7. Finding the inner flow

Find your inner peace through your mind's power. Place yourself in a comfortable spot, but try to avoid falling asleep. As you lay down, think or imagine your blood flowing through your veins around your body. Concentrate on one area at a given time, then shift in how it flows to another area. Keep this going for at minimum 5 minutes, and then 10 minutes until you've reached the maximum you're able to reach. This will allow you to become more conscious of your body's condition.

8. Mirror Trust

Sit in front of a mirror , and draw or place two marks within your eyes, which will be reflected in your reflection. Imagine yourself in the position of another's eyes. Imagine the other person as the person who you are most confident in and might be a family member or spouse, parent or sibling you know. Make sure you look at the marks as if were looking into the eyes the person you're picturing. If you are able to find the peace and calm in the other person, it is likely that you'll be relaxed and stress- free after this practice. Sometimes, it is just necessary to remember and know that you aren't alone in any issue we may face. This exercise is designed for people who are worried so excessively that it impedes their thinking.

9. Sifting Sound

The exercise can be completed anywhere at any moment. All you need is your hearing ability and your concentration. You can stay on the middle of a bustling street and filter sounds that are in the air. You might be able to identify the sounds of a particular vehicle and concentrate on it for 3 to 5 minutes. After that, switch your attention to a different sound. You could also sit in a café and be able to distinguish sounds sources too. You could be able to hear the grind of the coffee beans as they change to the cafe's music and after which you can listen to the conversations of the customers.

10. Word count

Take a book out and take a moment to count the words on the pages. Don't read or look at the words in your mind, just count. Continue doing this until your next page. Complete the counting as far as you are able to get. Challenge yourself. It may seem like a simple task, but we all know how easily get distracted. This exercise can help you to concentrate more evenly without having to speak about your thoughts.

Dietary Supplements for the Brain

One factor that can affect your lack of concentration is a poor diet. Insufficient and right amount of minerals, vitamins and other nutrients may prevent your brain from working properly. Think about how your brain's concentration is similar to a vital organ inside your body that needs to function each day. It is well-known that the loss of this organ can be damaging. That's why, as every other organ of the body, the mind to be able to be able to concentrate efficiently and effectively must be supplied by the correct and appropriate quantity of nutrition. A balanced diet is essential to improve your concentration.

The following brain foods are the best to boost the ability of your mind to concentrate during the entire day. Therefore, add these to your daily diet:

1. Oatmeal

Breakfast is the most important food item of the day especially when you have a lengthy day ahead. It is important to put your brain to the area by feeding it appropriate nutrition. Oatmeal is a fantastic source of energy but it has lower caloric content. If you're busy with a lot of tasks throughout the day, it is essential make sure you have a satisfying and satisfying breakfast. Oatmeal keeps you more full for longer, so you don't need to be concerned or be concerned about a fluctuating stomach while doing your work or trying to focus.

2. Dark Chocolate

Dark chocolate, in the correct quantity, that is one square portion, is sufficient to reap the benefits of your ability to concentrate. Dark chocolates are able to aid in the production of Serotonin as well as endorphins. These are neurotransmitters linked to improved concentration. Furthermore, the nutrients also help blood flow to the brain which makes cognitive processes like concentration, for instance, more efficient.

3. Water

The dehydration causes fatigue. When we're tired it is easy to finish all the work we have to accomplish and complete it without really focusing on it. This is why tasks are completed in low quality. The fatigue can affect our ability to concentrate and perform tasks effectively. Sometimes, the primary reason for this fatigue is due to dehydrated. Drink plenty of fluids to ensure that you are going with sufficient fuel. This way, you'll be tired less and can do more.

4. Blueberries

Blueberries aren't just great to snack on, but studies have demonstrated that they are memory enhancers since they boost the capacity of a person to concentrate and understand more.

5. Salmon

Salmons are rich in omega-3 fatty acids that help the body to rebuild cells, slow cognitive decline, and help improve the connectivity of your brain, particularly those related to memory and concentration. The protein in salmon that contains amino acids assist the brain in developing concentration and sharpness.

6. Coffee

Coffee aids by releasing norepinephrine within the body. It is a neurotransmitter which informs your body to remain awake. Once the body is able to be conditioned to stay in this level, it's capable of staying focused for a longer time spans already.

7. Green Tea

Green tea is a source of an amino acid known as Theanine. The amino acid has been proven to increase mental clarity and concentration. Green tea also has caffeine, which aids to release norepinephrine however, it's more healthy to drink than coffee, as coffee can have negative consequences in the long-term.

8. Beets

Beets contain high levels of nitrate which helps dilate blood vessels, boost the flow of blood in the body, as well as also transport oxygen into the brain thus improving mental performance and focusing ability.

9. Bananas

Bananas are widely known as potent potassium sources. Potassium is an important mineral to keep the heart, nerves and, more importantly the brain in top forms and working.

10. Spinach

Spinach has high levels of folate, lutein and beta-carotene. These nutrients are linked to preventing dementia, one of the conditions in which concentration is impaired. Spinach is a great brain food and can be used as a garnish to many recipes.

11. Eggs

Eggs are also a good source of sufficient omega-3 fatty acids which aid to improve your memory, and improving mood. Additionally, they have the chemical choline, which assists in keeping cells' membranes in the brain well-maintained.

12. Green Leafy Vegetables

The green leafy vegetables are abundant in fiber, as well as many other nutrients that help to maintain the energy levels of the body. If the body is in best energy levels, it can perform without having to worry about anxiety and fatigue, making the brain more involved in its focus.

13. Tomatoes

They are a great source of antioxidants which help cells in the brain to reduce inflammation and also increase the flow of blood and oxygen within the brain. These antioxidants can allow the brain to function at its best for cognitive function and focusing.

14. Meat Dairy

Dairy products from meat are good for your brain, but in small quantities. It is a rich source of B6 and B12 that can prevent memory loss and other problems with the brain from being developed (such as dementia and Alzheimer's). However, eating meat that comes from dairy products should be consumed to a moderate amount.

15. Avocadoes

Avocados are high in fiber, which aids in increasing the flow of blood within the body, allowing better transport of nutrients to organs, like the brain. Additionally, avocados can help to fill your stomach for longer. Therefore, if you're planning to do something for long periods of time throughout the day, it is advisable to take a bite of avocado prior to tackling the project.

16. Flax Seeds

Flax seeds are rich in B-Vitamins and Omega-3 fatty acids and fiber. All of these minerals and nutrients are vital to maintain mental clarity. They make one more capable of focusing and concentrate or pay attention. Flax seeds can be ground and sprinkled on your oatmeal, salad, or cereal.

17. Nuts

Nuts are high in vitamin E content, which is associated with a lower likelihood to cognitive performance as we age. You can eat nuts as snack or use them as small components in various recipes that you like.

A diet that helps the brain be able to concentrate effectively isn't an incredibly enjoyable task initially, however, if you consider yourself and decide to live an approach to life that values growth, productivity and physical activity, taking part in a brain food diet will not be that difficult to accomplish. Like self-regulation, participating in a diet that improves the brain's ability of concentrating better demands dedication, commitment and discipline. It won't be easy, but it's not impossible.

Chapter 5: Find A Place To Restore Your Mind Power

Sometimes, the thing that stops you from doing extremely well does not result from your inability to control your behavior, but instead it's the chaos that you're in. It is not just about having to control their self. This would be useless if one is unable to manage and control the surroundings in order to make it more conducive to concentration and concentrating.

Here are some suggestions to help you create conditions and an environment that will be conducive for concentration:

1. Find a quiet place

The first step is to choose a great workplace. It is important to think about several aspects when selecting a location is it quiet? Do I have the ability to stay motivated the area? Do I have enough time?

If you decide to go to a location ensure that the elements you're looking for are a part of the to the area. Sometimes, it is a matter of searching--you might have to go from one cafe to another until you locate the ideal one with a reasonable and delicious coffee, a reliable internet connection with a calm and peaceful environment, as well as an ideal working environment. You may also be able to hop from one library to the next until you locate one that's not packed and offers the services you may require. Find yourself your study or working area that will be ideal for you to focus and be productive.

2. Make sure you have everything you require

Do not get distracted by worrying about other things when you're working on something. Get all the things you'll require when you are studying or working. Take your notebook, notebooks markers, highlighters, pens papers, and the essentials. If you ever need these items, you don't need to spend time searching for them or bringing the items to your office. Your time is the most valuable resource when you are focused.

3. Find a spot that you can work from continuously

Once you've found the perfect place, make it a habit in the meantime. Finding the place that's motivating and inspire you to work hard can make you want to remain there. Don't be afraid to make a commitment to this location since the more you go to it to work it will become more familiar to your mind. gets used to the place as a signal to keep you focused. Think of this as a process of preparing your brain for be productive.

4. Set aside paper and a pen

Research has shown that having a pen and paper at the side of your workspace can help you stay focused on taking notes of your tasks and keep you in the right direction, and allowing yourself more engaged in your work. Keep notes while you work. The more tangible your notes are, the better they will stick to your mind.

5. Study or work in different ways

Being exposed to constant stimuli makes it boring. Whatever you think of it, no matter how you love a course but if it doesn't pose an obstacle to you, it's the same as a rag from the past. Therefore, to stop this growing boredom you must learn to diversify your routines and assignments.

Maybe you can assign different tasks to different times of the week, and then change them within two weeks or so. If you want, to enhance your study and work more engaging, even with only you. Don't get bored and look for strategies to keep your area of study more exciting and enjoyable.

6. Beware of temptations

Find a way to control your environment by keeping the safest away from all the temptations around you: electronic devices and other people, films and TV shows, the internet, and so on. It is also possible to include this into your list of criteria when searching for the best place to work from. One of the most effective ways to ensure you are productive is to stay clear from any possible tempting things that might take your focus.

Apart from self-care and diet, having the ideal work environment is an important aspect is considered in the event that one would like to be successful in paying attention to their work.

Finding the ideal spot for your business cannot occur overnight, or all at once. Furthermore, managing the environment so that it can make it more conducive to work is a daunting task since you will never truly grasp all the elements in the surrounding. However, this doesn't stop you from doing the best you can to make an environment that is conducive to your mind's power within its personal environment.

Chapter 6: Understanding The Various Components Of The Iq Test

Over the years thousands of individuals have looked for methods of precisely assessing their own personal levels of intelligence. Exams have been developed and research studies conducted throughout the years to attain this objective. Knowing the various components that comprise the IQ test can allow people to comprehend the reason why this particular test is an effective method to test your IQ.

The verbal portion focuses on the efficient use of the entire vocabulary. The ability to comprehend language and also being able to effectively convey one's own thoughts is a major aspect of this section. Analogies words, word grouping aswell in the identification of synonyms and antonyms for certain words are but a few topics covered.

The section on mathematics has the greatest emphasis on understanding the ability of one person to compute and their overall ability to perform basic math and geometry. While many of the problems which are discussed specifically require numbers, they'll require some type of mathematical calculation to be performed. This includes many series-related problems and math-related problems that need to be resolved.

The analysis of classification helps to clarify the way in which an assortment of items can be connected. The section that is highlighted, covering reasoning with logic tests the individual's understanding of causal and effect relationships. These are difficult to study for prior to taking the test.

In the section of spatial reasoning in the exam, the candidate's ability to control three-dimensional objects in variety of methods is extensively assessed. This requires the applicant to utilize their intelligence in the moment without the benefit of a thorough preparation and research. The assembly of various objects, the arrangement of different pictures, and creating specific block patterns are just a few things covered.

The visual perception region which is being studied focuses on how an individual process visual information as well as the conclusions they draw from what they've observed. Examining this area of intelligence lets one know their performance in terms of understanding information and the effectiveness they have in communicating with other people. Connecting distinct but related segments of information and being able recognize something that doesn't belong to a specific group is something that is investigated.

Numerous studies across the years have shown that the part that focuses on being able to recognize patterns is an essential component of the overall exam. People in everyday life must be able to sense order, even when their environment is in total chaos. The extent to which they are able to achieve this is being assessed within this segment.

While it might appear like an easy test but there are a variety of elements that comprise this IQ test that should be taken into consideration. Each of these parts focuses on a particular part of the mind of an individual that allows them to understand a range of issues that they will encounter every day. This is something anyone of all ages could benefit from learning about themselves, as well as the abilities you'll need to acquire to boost your intelligence.

What Can You Do To Identify Your Strengths and Strengths in Relation to Your IQ

Each person has their unique strengths, and they do not have to be tied to their IQ. But, people who are smart will make use of their strengths in a more efficient manner. Additionally, they'll be able to tackle their weaknesses making use of them to their advantage. Here are some suggestions on for identifying your strengths and weaknesses with regard to your intelligence.

Look around you. There are always those without any formal education that are more than competent in their job. They might not be capable of solving more complex math problems or achieve a impressive scores on the Mensa test but they can boast impressive achievements in other fields. They recognize their abilities and are using their skills in the most efficient method.

On the other hand there is at the very least one person who is extremely intelligent and well educated but still does not succeed in their life. The person may have all the qualities that are good however they don't know how to bring out the most of them.

What they are lacking is the ability to identify their strengths and make use of it to their advantage.

Find out how to better understand yourself. Grab a piece of paper and note down the things that naturally occur to you. Here are some suggestions of natural strengths you might possess.

The ability to think creatively, for instance. People who are creative have the capacity to tackle problems in different methods. If something can't be solved they'll figure out ways to solve it, and delight taking on a new task.

Social intelligence is extremely useful in every situation. The ability to understand the needs of others, their wants and motivations, and the ability to create a positive environment for various social interactions is highly attractive. Apart from that, this particular characteristic will provide a huge advantage in both the social as well as business.

Leadership is another highly regarded quality that is highly appreciated. Certain people have it naturally and do possess an exceptional charisma. They can make people respect them. Others can be excellent in the team, constantly contributing and being a an integral part of the group. Also, it is of high quality.

Be honest when answering these questions honestly. The process of becoming a better, more successful individual is up to you. Find out if you're happy as a team member or would you like to become a team leader.

Recognizing the strengths of an individual will be the initial step. It is important to improve these abilities and utilize them to your advantage. Also, you don't need to eliminate all your shortcomings, but knowing them can be an benefit.

Perhaps you don't know about certain qualities. Ask your family and friends to share their honest thoughts regarding you. You may be amazed by their responses. Perhaps they have a deeper understanding about you than they do about yourself. Perhaps they perceive yourself as a leader from birth and you're too shy to acknowledge that, not even to yourself.

These traits can affect how you perform when taking your IQ test. One way to discover what your weaknesses and strengths are to practice taking an IQ test or even the real test. When you receive the results you can see the areas you're naturally strong in and what areas you can enhance your performance.

One approach is to focus on the things you're already proficient in, something that probably isn't a natural thing to do and strive to build on that strength. The other option is to concentrate on your weakest scores and the section of the test and work to improve your abilities in that particular section. Whatever method you choose reviewing what you are good at and where it is weak will allow you to determine your study and making preparations for your IQ test.

If you are able to recognize your weaknesses and strengths regarding your IQ and IQ, you'll be more effective and more confident when taking tests because your test prep can be customized to the exam.

The Mind as a Muscle-Exercises, Ideas For Stretching Your Mind

Physical exercise is good for health, strengthens the body and increases endurance. This is the kind of exercise that people are accustomed to. Actually, when people hear the term exercise, they usually associate it with running and lifting weights. However, there's a an alternative type of exercise done to strengthen the brain. Exercise improves the mental areas of brain, such as critical thinking, creativity and reaction time, among other things. Once you begin to think of the mind as a muscular system exercising your brain become part of your daily routine.

One method to work your brain is to take part in games or tests designed to improve your brain's capabilities. These tests and games are available online for free. They can include speed tests that require you to press a button when something happens on screen or flashes. Also, there are games that test memory where you have to recall the things you've just presented to you within just a few seconds. Puzzles that require logic ask you to arrange or manipulate objects to get the desired results. There are a lot of websites offering these types of tests. You can visit them and then see how you fare.

If you don't have access to the web, you can find still methods to stimulate your brain. It is possible to read something that is challenging. This can help you create new connections in your brain. This is also true for filling mental puzzles like crosswords as well as Sudoku. According to research studies, having intellectual conversations in which you can present an argument that is well-thought out, listen to the views of the other person , and respond to opposing arguments will also increase your knowledge. This improves your mental agility and the ability to think critically.

Changes in habits can also help exercise the brain. If you're learning something, you should try doing it in a variety of ways. This can force your brain to work more to retain the knowledge. It also expands the reach of the brain's capabilities. It is also possible to make use of your hands that are less dominant to complete tasks. This is a very effective way to exercise. It stimulates the brain to create new nerve pathways , thereby increasing the brain's ability.

Try to do things while you're closing your eyes. Some examples of things you could do this method include showering and eating. The brain is forced to change and improves its ability to keep track of the place where things are.

Beware of staying in one location for a long time. Explore other areas. This stimulates your brain similar to how engaging and socializing with other people stimulates it. If you're in a different area, it's possible to discover new things that can aid in improving your abilities.

Do your best to master something new, such as the language or instrument. While you're doing it, brain cells grow as new pathways are created. This boosts the capacity and intelligence.

Take a sniff of different scents. Certain scents provide a calming sensation for the brain. One of them is rosemary. There is ongoing research conducted on specimens of the plant to determine this. This is a method of improving your problem-solving skills which won't cause harm to the fly. Try it out. test. Cooking can be an extremely beneficial exercise - smelling the various ingredients in the kitchen calms your mind and stimulates the brain. When you next go out shopping, take your nose out.

Write down any information you want to remember. This helps your brain in many ways. Writing is a way of giving instructions to your brain to determine what is important as well as what's not and, consequently, it helps you remember events more quickly when you come back. Scientists have found that writing is a great method to clear your mind. It's simply the best way to improve your thinking ability and creativity.

Play Mozart. In a research study, where the participants were youngsters who performed on the piano and sang and sung, it was concluded that the music helped them become proficient at solving problems.

Include fish in your diet. Fish consumption improves concentration and boosts neural transmissions. Research has proven that there is a near exact correlation between eating fish and lower levels of depression. The study further revealed how the findings were identical all over the world. There's a catch but not all types of fish produce the desired results. Salmon is the best choice. Consume other fish that have decent amounts of fat.

Try something simple like flipping pictures upside down. This causes the brain to be more focused when looking at them. This is one of the ways to boost your capacity of the brain. If you think of your mind as a muscle exercising to stretch your brain will help to improve your intelligence and memory.

What you need to know about using music to improve Your IQ

Utilizing music to boost your IQ is a breeze and can be done by anyone with just a few easy steps. Research studies have proven of the fact that listening to specific kinds of music , or performing certain instruments can boost the intelligence level of a person. It is crucial to remember that certain genres can reduce intelligence, rather than raising it, and therefore must avoid at all times for those who want to improve their intelligence.

A listening experience to classical music such as those composed by Beethoven as well as Mozart can lead the listener's mind through various distinct states that can't be reached through any other method. The frequency of the sound produced by instruments of music, such as violins, are distinct enough to enhance the intellect of an individual. After listening to classic music the intelligence level of the listener may be increased by five points.

The punk, rock and other genres have been proven to have a negative impact upon the brain. People who listen to these songs are believed to have a low intelligence percentage. This could be due to the degenerative effects the songs can are having on the brain. The music genres of rock and punk are generally chaotic and the frequency of sound created by the instruments are rarely in perfect harmony. The listening to of these songs will result in mental instability and a decrease of intelligence.

The connection between sound or audios and the brain is due to the fact that our brains resonate at the same frequency the music that a listener. When the frequencies are low, and soothing the brain can resonate at the same frequency, which makes it easier for the person to focus and absorb more information. This is the way to increase intelligence.

Certain musical instruments may enhance the attention span of those who use the instruments. The people who use the violin, harp , or trumpets in addition to other instruments are known to have higher intelligence. However people who play rock instruments are thought to have low IQ.

In addition to improving intelligence levels music can also assist people rest better. It also helps decrease depression, anxiety and aggressive behaviour. It may also help improve mood and concentrate. These will all contribute to general wellness which is the aim for every person.

Auditing specific songs regularly can help improve memory. Being able to remember things during tests is a crucial aspect of being able to achieve an excellent IQ score. Anyone who wants to achieve a high score should choose the best tunes to hear. There are numerous websites that offer playlists of songs that aid individuals in improving your memory and IQ and confidence in themselves.

Making use of music to increase your IQ is an affordable way to increase your ability to think. You might want to think about attending the Opera every once in awhile and watching Ballerinas dance and listen to classic music or other related activities. After a few months your IQ could have risen significantly by many points.

How to Make Use of Video Games As Well as Crosswords to increase your IQ

A lot of people ask what they can do to boost your memory. This chapter explains how you can make use of crosswords and video games to increase your intelligence. Engaging in games and working on puzzles can be beneficial as it can improve a person's memory. Who would have thought that getting more intelligent could be such enjoyable?

The IQ is a term used to describe intelligence quotient, is a way to measure the ability of a person to solve problems. It's mostly dependent on an individuals' auditory and visual abilities. People who are proficient in acquiring knowledge using these elements are reported to score better than those who are social and the olfactory learner.

The use of crosswords plays an important aspect in increasing the ability of a person to think and read. It allows people to increase their knowledge because they are encouraged to look up information that they didn't intend to prior to. The puzzles are created so that they are challenging for the players. It creates a sense of satisfaction for the players while they attempt to find an answer to the difficult and challenging areas.

The ability to solve puzzles with the hands that are not dormant also helps in the effort to train the brain. This can help stimulate the opposite part of the brain to the dormant hand. This makes it more functional and alert than it was prior to. Through engaging in this type of activity for a prolonged period of time people are likely to improve and enhance their abilities to see. It is also recommended to write more than normal activities like sending an unwritten letter in contrast the email method.

Video games is vital for exercising the brain. For instance, players are required to think and respond quickly to difficult situations. This creates a more thrilling game and stimulates your brain to become attentive and effective.

As players become more adept in their game their brains are able to function independently of glucose, which is the fuel for its functions. The game demands players to be on their feet constantly and this increases their alertness levels.

The majority of events require an individual to be aware of the things is happening. This can help increase concentration levels and memory. Because creativity and logic are an essential component when participating in these games the participants will need to improve how they judge and evaluate situations from the real world. Many scientists advocate the game-based approach to seeking to boost brain activity, as the outcomes and rewards are impressive.

Parents are thus encouraged to let their children play in their spare time. The more games they play, the more enjoyable as they face various problems and scenarios. Therefore, it is crucial to be aware of how important it is to engage in these techniques so that rewards can be reaped.

When determining how to utilize crosswords and video games to boost your IQ Individuals are encouraged to make these practice a routine. Making a crossword during lunch breaks can be useful after a particular time. The majority of participants have seen improvements in their ability to conceptualize concepts.

The Cryptology and Logic Puzzles to Increase Your IQ

It is the case that solving puzzles can improve your brain. The IQ is thought of as a measure of the ability to solve problems. Although your IQ is believed to be innate to the abilities you're naturally skilled at, you can make use of logic puzzles and cryptology to increase your IQ. The intelligence quotient isn't in fact a reliable measure of intelligenceby its own. It's actually a gauge of specific abilities and forms of learning.

People who have the highest IQs tend to excel in learning with auditory and visual abilities. The ability to master these two areas will be more accessible for those who are naturally predisposed to these skills. Even the case that you naturally excel in different ways, it's still possible to get more familiar with these techniques. When it comes to solving puzzles it is possible to improve your performance. One approach, particularly is to purchase magazines which print puzzles.

These could be newspapers or magazines, or you could purchase a magazine that is specialized in the subject. There are many options to pick from here, but the most well-known is Sudoku as well as crosswords. These games will assist you in learning by doing them frequently. It can help you master the subject faster. Your brain is stimulated when you get better at. Be confident that you're not able to master anything at first.

After some time and practice, you'll be able to tackle more difficult tasks. There are times when you will prefer one kind of puzzle over the other or focusing on what you consider to be more enjoyable is more likely to stimulate you. However it is recommended to solve the types you don't like as much, occasionally it will assist you.

It's even better to do these tasks alongside other kinds of puzzles. The logic and lateral puzzles are a huge advantage when you work on them. You may be unable to complete the task initially but you'll get better as you advance. Code breaking, or cryptology is a different method of problem-solving that could assist you. The purpose of this is try to decode codes that might, eventually let you know the message.

To do this, you'll have to search for patterns within the code. One thing you may find yourself doing is learning methods to assist you in solving problems and apply these in the subsequent. This is a way of learning and stimulating your mind.

Because of this you're getting more proficient in the abilities, yourself. Utilizing the methods and strategies you've learned means that tasks that were previously difficult are now becoming simpler.

It also enhances your capacity to learn since you can apply the methods you've learned to study new ways of doing things. Of course, this will assist you significantly, when learning about new subjects all around. In terms of using logic puzzles and cryptology to boost your IQ generally you have now the knowledge to take any exam.

The Art of Writing to stimulate your mind and thoughts Patterns

Most people do not know about the art of writing to increase your brain's energy and thinking patterns. The magic that is involved in writing an essay should not be missed at any time in time. This is because the entire procedure can improve your intelligence. If someone is deeply thinking about the word combinations they can make use of, their mind is stimulated in various ways. Over time, the brain's abilities are honed to the point where one can think at a moment's notice about various issues in life.

The main point is that writing is a part of our fundamental mental abilities. So, writing sentences that are logical is a practice that can bring benefits over the long run. In the short-term it is apparent that you are just engaging in a pastime that involves writing about life experiences or the way a person's mind is shaped by diverse life-related issues.

The best part about this sport is that it can be enjoyed by someone who is naturally gifted with words. Even those who aren't skilled writers can learn the art by writing their own thoughts repeatedly. There is no set formula to write. All a person needs to do is begin typing any thought that pops into mind and then the rest is history.

The rapid writing process makes it an essential instrument of IQ development. Since everything takes place in real-time beginning the moment you write the first sentence, it is reliable to conclude that an individual's thinking patterns will improve as time passes. The brain of a fanatic author is analogous in a few way to the processing on a functional computer. This is because it recalls information that was previously read within a matter of seconds.

The analytical aspect of writing is what stimulates our minds. It's a huge mistake to think that writers are people who slacks off in order in a meaningful way. The writer typically uses every aspect of his brain in the process of writing pieces of writing.

It is believed by many people that writing or playing music can have an impact on your mind. It is important to note that bringing a collection words to life isn't a way to be considered a success. Anyone who is able to master this ability will also have developed their general thinking patterns.

The mental aspect of writing is not a separate process. In reality, the entire thing links the recall function to the creative aspect of the human being as well as the other IQ aspects. These crucial connections can be useful in order to enhance thinking abilities.

To become an effective thinker and solve problems in a quick way, one needs to be aware of the importance of writing in order to stimulate your brain and thinking patterns. The results of these studies show that any activity that requires creative thinking can influence thought patterns positively. Over time the brain's capabilities is able to improve dramatically.

The Benefits of Performing Daily Brain Memory Exercises

Engaging in daily brain memory exercises can be a fantastic method of preparing the brain for higher performance. Like every other part of your human body, the greater you test and exercise your brain, the more it can respond to new types of stimuli as well as new issues. The effort will improve your mental acuity , making you much more capable to provide quick and insightful solutions to the most difficult problems that arise.

Here are a few more reasons to get your mind now. The earlier you begin working towards warding off the disease of Alzheimer's the more efficient you'll be. This is accomplished by ensuring that your brain is supplied with oxygen through regular and challenging exercises for the cardiovascular system and also by testing your mind with a series puzzles, as well as other tasks which require more complex thinking. Engaging your brain in a concentrated and intense way is similar to performing several sets of mental push-ups.

Enhancing your memory today can have its benefits. There is no need to wait until later phases of your life to experience the positive results you can achieve through these exercises. There are a variety of situations where people can benefit with a functioning memory.

In business, for instance it's never an excellent idea to not remember names of key contacts and colleagues. However, many people do it every day. It can lead to awkward conversations, and miss opportunities to effectively close deals. Many people think that they're not good at remembering names, instead of assuming that they've never had the time to help their brains to operate at the highest levels.

A clear memory is an excellent way to maintain an excellent relationship with your love interest. Instead of reliving every memorable moment that your partner will remember and treasures, you could begin to file these important dates too. Even though you may never have had great recall in your past doesn't mean you have to live all of your life in this manner. Exercise can enhance this part of the brain significantly.

There are a variety of other factors to take into consideration there is the fact that these efforts could increase your IQ. This means that you'll in fact be smarter and much more adept at thinking in the face of new difficulties. This could be that if the brain is challenged, it will improve itself.

Certain lifestyle choices can hinder being successful when trying to achieve gains in mental performance by utilizing specific exercises. For example, if you use tobacco products regularly or drink alcohol, they will limit the supply for oxygen into the brain. Inactivity and a unhealthy eating habits can affect the health of this region as well.

There are numerous benefits to doing daily brain-training exercises. If you are looking to get the maximum benefit from any aspect of this process you should also follow the correct nutritional exercises in addition. This will help ensure that the body's topmost organs are well-nourished. the body, which will ensure the most efficient transmission of information.

Extending Your Vocabulary to Improve Your IQ

Although many believe the notion that IQ is something is inherent to you the ability to expand your vocabulary to boost your IQ is an alternative. You can boost your the intelligence level simply by studying new terms. In addition to making your score increase, but you'll also transform the way people view you.

Others have impressions about youbased on the way you communicate and how you compose yourself. If you can learn and comprehend more words, you appear more intelligent. This boosts your confidence in your daily life, and also in interviews for jobs and other important events.

It is believed that the primary difference between students at the top and lowest in the school is smarter students possess a vocabulary of approximately five thousand words greater that their less IQ counterparts. This is an excellent sign that the words you are familiar with have an effect on your intelligence scores. The fact that you are more knowledgeable about words can help you comprehend the world around you and let you express yourself more effectively.

There are many advantages to having the ability to broaden the range of words you'll be using. It is easier to do well in your studies if you know more. This is a major benefit since you don't have to search for everything. Also, you will find that people will take your work more seriously, especially when you're capable of spelling these words.

It may at first appear daunting to increase your list of words by several thousand words.

The key is to start with a slow pace and then grow. It's possible to do this faster using specialized software, however If you're looking to learn more naturally, there are simple techniques that anyone can follow.

Consider getting an Word of the Day calendar which you can review each day. You can read it, speak it and then attempt to use the word in the form of a sentence. You can write it down several times, and ensure that you discover a way to apply it several instances throughout the course of your life. This will help to cement the concept into your mind.

Another approach is to go through your dictionary and make a an inventory of words that you don't really are familiar with. Pick a couple of words for each day and then go through them in the same manner as you would with a daily calendar word. The amount of words you choose to use will be contingent on the number you are at ease with and the number you are able to learn in a day. Keep the list in your pocket and check it at the at the end of each week.

To test your memory and find out whether the words are actually stuck, check the list every week. Spend a few minutes recollecting the definition and put the word in the form of a sentence. This is especially effective when you are able to collaborate with a friend and challenge one another. The idea of having the words written on cards also helps.

The ability to expand your vocabulary and improve IQ is something that everyone is able to do, no matter the level of their education. By adding a few more words every week can eventually help you reach that goal. It's much more simple than you imagine, and you won't be disappointed.

Enhance Problem Solving Skills Using Scenario Flashcards

There are many methods to enhance your IQ One is to increase your ability to solve problems. One way to stimulate your brain is to improve your problem-solving abilities by using flashcards that simulate situations.

It is the first thing to do: increase confidence in yourself. When you are thinking strategically and acting smart, you are more effective. It is recommended to always praise your effort at whatever you do even if you've not been successful. If you're trying to solve a problem by focusing on positive thoughts, it assists you in thinking clearly. If you are in a state of panic and overwhelmed, it affects your thinking and thinking processes. Remaining calm and composed when faced with a dilemma can boost your capabilities.

Purchase a set of flashcards that are based on scenarios or creative cards. They are available on the internet. They offer diverse scenarios, philosophies, or challenges for each one. Consider an actual issue. Take the card and study the strategies provided. What are the ways you can use this strategy to tackle the issue? Record all of ideas that cross your head.

If you'd like to take this activity one step further, you can use these cards in groups. Each person should present a scenario for the problem they wish to resolve. Then, they should discuss the problem and then choose a few cards and discuss how each card of philosophy can solve the issue. Discussions will generate the development of new ideas, patterns of thought and ways on things. It is possible to intensify the activity by putting the time limit. Each participant is given three minutes to come up with a solution and then as a group , choose the most effective resolution. Reduce the time to just one minute. This technique can train your brain to respond quickly and effectively to solve any problem.

Keep these cards inside your wallet, maybe inside your glove compartment. If you find yourself waiting somewhere, take them out and start looking through the cards. Invigorate your mind with different scenarios and think about how you can enhance or solve the problem with the techniques that are on the cards. Evaluation of options is that lets you choose the best strategy to tackle the problem. It can be achieved by the use of trial and error by experimenting with random guesses and various strategies.

You can locate these kinds of cards on the internet searching for a brainstorming card decks, or even an idea card deck. They can open your mind to the various options and methods for problem-solving. This will assist you in you take the IQ test and help you see challenges from different perspectives.

Invigorating your brain and increasing your IQ can be achieved through these exercises and the concepts inside this publication. Contrary to popular opinion the brain is actually an muscle that can be built, expanded and enlarged in time. It is not a matter of being born intelligent or dumb. If you're looking to improve you IQ score, do something and get your mind working. You'll begin to see impressive results and discover many opportunities for your personal growth.

Chapter 7: The Effects Of Brain Training And The Facts Of Neuroplasticity

The human brain is thought to be among the most intricate structures in the universe. It is the only brain that has the ability to create a certain level of intelligence and consciousness that is unlike any other animal has the capacity to possess.

The way that it generates consciousness and processes huge quantities of data is something scientists are unable to comprehend, despite the current technology and research methods. But, it is a testament to how powerful the human brain is.

How strong is your brain? By reading this book, you've demonstrated one of the most vital qualities of intelligence: curiosity. It's a human characteristic which is extremely helpful in the initial stage of learning.

If this is the case you're likely to be curious about the way your brain functions and may be seeking ways to improve your brain. However, first, you have to be aware of the distinction between knowledge, intelligence and wisdom.

The difference between intelligence knowledge, wisdom, and intelligence

The real difference between intelligence, knowledge and wisdom is fairly easy. The first thing to note is that knowledge is the term used to define the amount of useful information one has in various disciplines like math, science as well as psychology, language and the like. In a sense memory of a person can be considered to be knowledge. However, wisdom is the capacity to use information as well as knowledge and experience acquired over time to make good choices and "intelligent" ideas. In the end Intelligence is a characteristic that includes knowledge as well as wisdom.

Although it is believed that going to college is a sure way to increase your the level of intelligence, this isn't always the reality. Let's suppose a student studying law is able to graduate after several years of dedication and study. Although it's certain that he's accumulated the knowledge he gained through his education, he will need experience to gain knowledge and also a bit of both to increase his cognitive power and intelligence.

It is also believed that the capacity to attain wisdom, knowledge and intelligence is limited to the limits of a brainpower. This implies that some individuals have more capacity to achieve intelligence more than others. Factors like the size of their brain and genetics are believed to play a part in the determination of this. However, studies have shown that the power of your brain can be altered through the concept of neuroplasticity.

Neuroplasticity

Neuroplasticity, often referred to as cortical mapping or brain plasticity, is the brain's capacity to grow and become more flexible through real-world learning experiences. It works by changing the brain's structure, function and chemically. This means that your degree of brainpower that is the basis of your knowledge as well as your intelligence and knowledge can be cultivated through specific exercises for brain training using neuroplasticity.

In the context of neuroplasticity the brain adjusts its abilities based on a individual's needs. It's based on the specific way the brain manages and stores information that is new.

For instance, whenever you master the new skills the brain creates new neural pathways which contain the information necessary to master this new ability.

The good thing about neuroplasticity is that it's acknowledged to occur at any time - thereby denying the notion that changes to the brain only occur during childhood, and then cease completely after the age of adulthood. This is due to the fact that the human brain has been proven to continually develop new neural connections every time it is exposed to new learning environments. However, the changes that occur aren't always positive. Neuroplasticity is a concept that states the quality of the stored information may decrease in time as neural pathways weaken.

Introduction to neuroplasticity-based exercises

The research on neuroplasticity and how it can be improved is being developed until today. What research and evidence have revealed to date is that brain power can be increased through regular mental exercises known as "brain-training exercises".

These brain exercises target specific cognitive skills like concentration, attention, short-term and long-term memory, arithmetic capabilities as well as visual perception and many more.

Exercises for brain training are called non-invasive because they don't require any additional substances or drugs to be effective. They are based on providing the brain regular tasks and opportunities to develop and grow with neuroplasticity.

When it comes to brain-training exercises are concerned software programs are regarded to be among the most efficient. These programs are specifically created to focus on cognitive abilities that are necessary for gaining knowledge as well as wisdom and. The good news is that there are many websites that provide these programs for brain training online at no cost.

Information on these programs and other everyday tasks will be provided at times throughout this book. The main thing to remember for now is to prepare the required preparations to achieve the best results.

Preparation for Brain Training

Sharpening your brain and training your mind can open numerous opportunities for you in your daily life. Think about the various skills you can learn and all the people you will encounter, every adventures to experience and all the money to be earned. You are able to excel in your field, stand at ahead of your peers in the business world, and be the top in the field of your passion.

Another amazing thing that the human brain has is the capacity to accomplish whatever it is focusing on. It is all you need is the mental capacity, drive, and the capacity to focus on the goals you have set. You will also require the right conditions and everything could be possible.

In the present world of fierce competition the opportunities to improve your living standards can be offered to everyone. You'll need all the benefits that you can. For now you must think about these opportunities and make the objectives.

Setting your Objective: Why do desire more brainpower?

If you were to be asked "what could you possibly do, if you were the most brilliant person in the world" What would you tell them?

Every person has their own set of dreams and goals It's your responsibility to determine what yours is. This is extremely helpful in finding the motivation and perseverance required to be successful in your brain-training as well as to establish routines and habits that will maximise the power of your brain power.

A personal journal can be extremely useful throughout the book. It will assist you to set goals as well as creating routines and keeping track of your performance. You can utilize an actual notebook and personal computers to type your journal. However, for the moment you must figure out the reason why you should train your brain.

To assist you in getting started, you can consider these questions:

Are you slipping behind in your work and are looking for ways to make improvements?

Are there any particular people that you'd like to impress with your sharpening of mind?

Are you looking to learn the latest skill, but it's just too much for you?

Are you experiencing an increase in your memory, or other cognitive functions that you would like to enhance?

Are you stressed and you can't stop?

The answers to these questions will assist you in choosing the type of brain-training exercises you should follow and what routines you should be following in the near future.

the Factors of Intelligence Factors of the Brain

The primary functions of the brain that influence a person's total brain's performance can be classified into 6 distinct categories. These include a person's cognitive emotions, behavior and physical (physical) perception and signals. But, you'll be focusing on five reclassified fields of brain training exercises, including the logic, perception and calculus, language and memory.

Memory It is an important aspect in the development of your brain's overall power. The book you'll be working to improve the three types of memory (sensory long-term, short-term and long-term) with a variety exercises.

Perception - Your perception is an essential cognitive function that helps you manage the sensory inputs from your surroundings. It's the gateway to every learning experience that depend on your focus, concentration as well as alertness and attention.

Your problem-solving abilities and your capacity to draw valid conclusions based on data is the basis of your logic. Logic is a tool to improve a person's reasoning abilities as well as deductive abilities, and the ability to discern what data is reliable and which are false.

Language- This cognitive capability covers more than the capacity to talk. It also affects the person's emotional and behavioral thoughts. It also describes an individual's ability to connect letters, symbols and words to fully developed thoughts and concepts.

Calculus Achieving a reliable calculus does not mean that someone is proficient in math formulas, as the memorization of formulas like these requires the use of both your memory and calculus capabilities. In fact, this aspect of intelligence is determined entirely by your capacity to understand mathematical equations and mathematical questions. There may be a gap in your knowledge of the exact formulas to answer certain mathematical problems however, it will be a lot simpler for you to discover the solution. Calculus skills can be improved through training your memory, as well as increasing your accuracy by practicing.

Specific brain training exercises require at least one of the intelligence elements mentioned above. Your task now is to work on developing these specific intelligence elements each one at a time.

Getting Started

In your journal, write a note to you describing why you are taking exercise for brain development and your desired final results. You can write anything you like provided it's relevant to your motives in the field of brain training. This can also help you concentrate on a specific problem when you have one as one of your reasons.

It is important to note that this exercise is not just about determining and define your goals, you also perform an exercise that is a warm-up using your language skills in addition to observational abilities and focusing.

All you need to do is done!

Following the above activity You are now able to begin taking brain-training exercises that focus on a specific cognitive function. Make sure to keep your notebook in a safe place and not allow anyone else to read it.

Brain Training Strategies for Unparalleled Concentration

Concentration is a result of a person's perseverance, motivation willpower, determination as well as mental clarity. It also can help a person to learn faster, perform more effectively, and behave more efficiently by paying close attention to everything that is important.

When you are thinking about brain-training exercises, enhancing your concentration is the best method to begin.

Strategies to Improve your concentration

Concentration is extremely beneficial to improve your brain's performance over the long term. However, there is an important aspect you need to know about improving your focus - trying to concentrate too much is not going to help you concentrate.

Concentration is a learned ability and can only be learned through continuous training using the correct techniques. While it is possible to be temporarily boosted during work through various methods but it won't be as effective as educating your ability to concentrate on an independent task.

Concentration is dependent on your ability to stay clear of distractions that hinder your ability to concentrate initially.

For a breakthrough in concentration and to make use of its benefits over the long term, attempt the following workouts:

1. The practice of counting backwards is probably the easiest and quickest way to improve your attention. It's also a good warming up before starting any other brain-training exercises. For the beginning, begin from ten , and count down to one. Then, you can begin counting down from 20. Continue the process until you have completed it; gradually increasing your number to the

highest level you are able to. Note your progress in your personal journal , and then try to beat your record on the next session.

2. The Advanced Backward Counting - It is the difficult version of the previous. When counting backwards beginning from ten, you can skip 3 numbers when you count. For instance, add 10, 7, 4 1, and finally 20 17 14 11 9 6 3,0. Keep increasing the first number as high as you can. Remember to record your scores in your journal, and attempt to beat it in future attempts.

3. Quick Sensory Stimulation are able to pay for professional stimulation sessions, such as music therapy, aromatherapy massage, and more. However, you can also do your own fast sensory stimulation

Exercise at exercise at home. The sensorimotor memory of an individual is responsible for processing information for a very small amount in time (less than 1 second). This kind of memory will be described in more detail in Chapter 4. The exercise should begin with the following items such as any music player (iPod Cell phone, iPod, etc.) or any flavor of non-alcoholic beverage (tea lemonade, hot cocoa and so on.) or any other book. It is the next thing to do: locate and sit in the most comfortable chair at your home. Make sure you are in a position that you have access to all the items without stepping on the chair. Then, you can take a break and concentrate on enjoying many things at once. The final step is to write down every experience (the flavor or the taste of the beverage, tune that played or playing, etc.) on your journal in short sentences.

4. Simple Meditation Exercise - Unlike traditional meditation that usually requires a cushion and incense Simple meditation can be done anywhere and in any position. Start with closing your eyes, and then visualizing an iron box. Then, for the next five minutes take anything that pops out of your head inside the box and then close it. After that, concentrate on the box that is closed for 5 minutes or so until you feel completely relaxed.

Keep in mind that the best time to perform the above exercises is in the free time, and not when doing an a crucial job. If you do this, it will cause you to lose focus on the task. It takes time to improve your focus however it's quite easy to achieve results quickly.

Training to improve your focus can take just a few minutes each to complete and are therefore effortless to incorporate it into your routine. Be sure to keep track of any improvements in your journal to help decide which one works best for you.

Mind Clarity Training and Focus

Your mental clarity, concentration and focus all are essential to learning and experience. While focus and concentration help you to prioritize your work when it comes to mentally challenging tasks, mental clarity can improve the quality of the information you acquire and also the quality the work you produce.

Random-number Sequence Training

This simple workout helps you develop your ability to focus on an arithmetic activity while increasing your memory to recall the sequence of numbers. It can help keep your brain alert and focused even after hard work.

To begin, you can start by declaring three single digit numbers. For example, declare 2 - 7 - 8. Next, you must declare these numbers exactly in the same sequence with a new digit every time. For instance you could declare 2 7 - 7 8 - 5, and then 2 - 7 - 8- 5 2. Continue to do this until you're unable to remember the exact sequence of numbers. You might be surprised by the number of numbers you are able to remember by adding each digit one at a time. This is a demonstration of the capacity for the brain's ability to organize data with ease, especially when the data is entered one by one. The training in the Random-number sequence can be done by a partner. Just take turns creating and expanding the sequence. This makes the exercise difficult and more effective.

Memory Improvement and Building A Photogenic Memory Through Brain Training

A memory that isn't working is one of the most annoying consequences of a weak brain. Think about how often you've walked into the room only to forget the things you're supposed to be doing or forgetting where you put the keys to your car or forgetting an crucial task because you're busy with other things. What happens if you begin not forgetting but instead remembering?

Imagine how much easier your life could be if the opposite was the case. Imagine if you suddenly remembered the contact numbers of your important contacts or answers to an extremely important exam at school?

The power of a person's memory is a crucial factor in the process of learning. When you improve your concentration,

The Memory Works the Memory Works

There are three primary kinds of memory that are found within the brain of humans. the short-term memory and the long-term memory, and sensory memory.

The order in which the newly stored information in brain in the following order:

Sensory memory - short-term memory Long-term memory

Basic information derived from the person's senses (taste and touch, smell as well as hearing, sight and smell) is automatically detected by sensors. The sensory memory serves as a filter that determines what information is important and what isn't.

The relevant information is stored in a person's short-term memory or active memory. The short-term memory is in close contact with the working memory of a person that plays a crucial role in the brain's consciousness and capabilities.

Finally, a piece of data can be saved in the long-term storage memory only after it has been processed by the short-term memory. The memory that is long-term is capable of keeping information for a long time. In addition, the long-term memory is split into two types called the declarative and procedural memory.

The declarative memory may be split into two subtypes , known as the episodic memory and the semantic memory. The episodic memory is a repository of details that a person has acquired through real-world experiences. For instance, the memories of your birthday celebration is recorded as episodic memories. However semantic memory stores the truth and popular notions. For instance, understanding the difference between a cat versus an raccoon can be stored in semantic memory.

Another type of memory that is long-lasting, called the procedural memory stores information on motor functions and patterns that have been developed through practice and experience. The procedural memory can also be known as muscles memory implicit memory, body memory. Learning to walk, jog or even ride the bicycle are examples of procedural memory.

To summarise the relation between the different types of memory each type of memory is contingent on the high quality sensory memory that is acquired.

The sensory memory of your brain is where the other types of memory will start. The quality of a memory that is long-term depends on how well the short-term memory is integrated in your brain. Furthermore, the quality of the information you acquire from your short-term memory depends on the quality of the information accumulated from the sensory memories you have. In addition, the quality of the information gathered by your sensory memory is contingent on your attention and concentration of your learning experience.

This is the reason that improving your ability to focus and concentrate first is vital to brain training. Remember to continue practicing your concentration and focus capabilities by doing the exercises from the preceding chapter. They are extremely beneficial to maximize the effectiveness of the remaining exercises included in this book.

Memory Exercises

Memory loss can happen with time as they get older. It is possible to prevent this by following a healthy diet and doing simple daily routines to improve the memory. Here are some routines that will fit into anyone's routine:

1. Journal Writing: Every every night before bed, make a note in your personal journal of important events that took place throughout the day. Be sure to write like you're writing to yourself in the near future. Try to write as many words as you can over 20-30 minutes. Do this each day. This simple activity helps improve your memory by enhancing your capacity to remember and visualize short-

term events that will be reinforced during rest.

2. Quick Reading Comprehension In order to improve your short-term memory, must expose it to as many challenges that you are able to. Find the closest book to you and go through its contents. It doesn't matter what type of book you have, however it's much better to get an informative book, such as the science textbook. Make sure you read at least 10 paragraphs, without having to stop or go back through previous paragraphs. Write in your journal everything you've learned from what you've just read. Check how accurate your quick-term memory the words you wrote against

the information you the information you. This is an efficient way to study for exams.

3. Engage in Brain Games - Mentally challenging games like chess scrabble and Sudoku are known to offer sufficient amounts of brain stimulation that keep the brain alert. In a study that involved students from 4,000, four months playing with chess demonstrated significant improvements on the IQ of players who played often. The great aspect of this

game is the fact that they're enjoyable to play, especially with a partner. Be aware that spending long hours spent playing these games won't give greater results than playing for just a few minutes per day.

Memory Strategies

Be aware that the quality of your memory depends on a variety of aspects of your life, aside from the fact that you are doing exercise for your brain. To maintain your sharp memory and to protect against possible decline it is essential to maintain an active, healthy and balanced way of life.

1. It is important to sleep on time. Humans are designed to rest in the night time for a reason. In the beginning, your body is in an internal process of self-repair which addresses any damage, regulates hormones and conducts detoxification processes. Additionally, REM (Rapid-eye movement) sleep can improve the quality of memory long-term by increasing the flow of blood to specific regions of the brain that are responsible to process memories. This is why it's essential to maintain a regular and healthy

sleep schedule for keeping your brain in top shape and in good shape.

2. Eat Right Like any other organ within your body, your brain depends extensively on oxygen and blood to function. This is why certain types of foods that boost oxygen circulation and blood flow are believed to play a significant role on the cognitive performance. Some examples of these foods that are beneficial to the brain include fish (sardines mackerel, tuna, mackerel and salmon supplements with fish oil and more.), vegetables (beet, spinach, carrots, broccoli, etc.), fruits (blueberries, apples, bananas, apricots, etc.) as well as green tea as well as red wine.

Brain Training Websites

As increasing numbers of people are aware of the benefits of training their brains increasing numbers of brain-training websites are popping up on the internet to cater to the ever-growing demand. Some of the sites provide paid services for regular brain exercises, other websites like NeuroNation provides users with a range of brain training exercises that are simple.

1. Brain Arena

2. Sharp Brains

3. BrainHQ

4. Brain Metrix

5. Lumosity

Stress, Habit-Forming , and Brain Training

Training for brains is more than doing exercises to activate the brain. A major aspect of brain training is understanding how to manage stress, which can cause a variety of cognitive difficulties.

Stress isn't an actual health issue. It's your body's normal reaction when confronted with triggers and dangerous situations like public speaking, work tasks workplace, environmental pollution, the loss of a loved ones, and other such. When stress is present to the brain, it sends nerve signals that trigger an increase in adrenaline levels.

These hormones can increase your body's blood pressure and heart rate to allow the body to react faster. However, stress can turn risky when it is accumulated over time. It can increase the risk of heart attack or stroke and weakens the immune system.

The modern stress-free life is nearly impossible. However, there are a variety of methods to manage stress and reduce it.

The reduction of stress by reducing the accumulation

Stress is something you likely encounter daily. It could happen at your workplace, home or even in time with acquaintances.

When it comes to brain training is concerned Stress can result in these cognitive issues:

1. Poor decision-making

2. Unawareness

3. Memory issues

4. Negative thinking

5. Anxiety

To avoid stress from developing at work, you should follow these strategies:

The 90-minute work day

It is vital to realize that the brain can perform at its peak efficiency for about 90-120 minutes. According to Nathan Kleitman, the "basic rest-activity cycle" is a 90-minute cycle which can be observed during the course of a person's work during the daytime. This pattern shows that the brain is working in a particular alertness pattern known as"the ultradian rhythm. When you understand the 90-minute cycle It is recommended to take 20-minute breaks following each 90 minutes of intensive work. This will ensure that you work to your maximum effectiveness every single time while preventing stress from building up.

Drinking Coffee

The majority of offices have coffee-makers due to the reason. Caffeine is a very potent wakefulness-promoting agent that provides a quick boost of alertness - helping millions of people across the globe complete menial and boring tasks. Coffee is also believed to possess powerful antioxidants that make it ideal to drink regularly, as much as 3 times per day. In a research conducted by the

University of Sussex, drinking tea or coffee was ranked third as the top stress relieving activity, following listening to music or reading an ebook. Be aware that drinking excessive coffee consumption can cause adverse side effects like anxiety, heartburn and insomnia.

Negative Thinking and Productivity

The ability to increase productivity is one of the primary objectives of brain training. If you keep your mind in tip-top shape and sharp, you're actively preparing yourself to reach and increase your time productively. But anxiety, stress, negativity and procrastination can keep you from benefiting from brain training.

As a vital component of brain development, now is the time to work on some well-known obstacles particularly negative thinking and procrastination.

Most often, negative thinking stems from the fear of negative results. In many instances the anticipation is not justified and more likely to be the result of a inability to plan and the inability to set goals. With a good dose of optimistic energy, can take you a long distance.

Physical Exercise

Engaging in regular physical activities is proven to relieve stress and keep your brain healthy over the long term. It is because physical exercises boost your body to produce endorphins. Endorphins can trigger positive emotions like satisfaction and happiness. They also function as an effective natural pain reliever and is extremely beneficial in alleviating anxiety.

There is no need to engage in intense workouts if you only need to increase the effectiveness from brain-training. Here's a list of exercises with low intensity that you can carry out each day:

1. Jogging

2. Cycling

3. Swimming

4. Skipping Rope

Organizing your Lifestyle

In order to aid in the brain training exercises you can do as well as fight negativity and procrastination It's the perfect time to refresh and plan your calendar. Use the steps below to determine your goals in the near future:

1. Make a schedule for the week by calculating your time off in between daily obligations like sleeping, working and eating.

2. You can make the most of your spare time by incorporating the various exercises for brain training you've found through this publication. Around 2 hours of daily brain exercises are enough.

3. Make sure to incorporate physical exercises into your routine to maximize effectiveness.

4. Be sure to establish weekly goals to ensure you're spending you time in the most efficient method you can.

Neuro Linguistic Programming For Beginners

Neuro-Linguistic Programming (also known as NLP)is a method of communication and learning created in the late 1970s by John Grinder and Richard Bandler in the year 1975. It is a complicated learning system that has assisted numerous people to master specific skills using NLP techniques and mindsets.

The benefits the effects Neuro-Linguistic Programming are best described as a complete improvement in all aspects about an individual. Additionally, the techniques of Neuro-Linguistic Programming are distinct because they mostly relie on the stimulation of sensations - somewhat similar to self-hypnosis.

This chapter will concentrate on Neuro-Linguistic Programming to aid in brain training.

Basic Neuro-Linguistic Programming

Anchoring

Anchoring is an extremely basic but highly effective method to boost self-confidence and motivation. With Anchoring, an individual can imagine a particular positive situation or "positive emotions at their peak". This will be linked to a particular trigger using Neuro-Linguistic Programming.

Anchoring can be a great practice for developing all kinds of memory, from short-term to sensory. It's also a great option to ease stress and increase concentration during stressful times.

So, the positive feelings will be readily accessible in the future through the trigger you set. To accomplish it, you must follow the following easy steps:

1. Select a particular memory. The memory should bring powerful positive emotions. Be sure to ensure that this memory is something you are confident in doing, such as playing your instrument of choice or playing your favorite childhood game with your friends or playing with your favorite child.

2. Relive the experience - With your imagination, try to imagine the memory as vividly that you are able to. Make the memory appear large and try to remember every single visual element particularly the hue. Try to recall other aspects of your senses in the present scene such as an odor, contact, or sound. Try to experience the high levels of positive emotions at the peak in intensity and keep it going for a period of time.

3. Connect the Anchor - When you feel that the memory has the highest emotional

intensity then you are prepared to anchor it. The first step is to relive the experience again, starting at the beginning. While doing this, begin to trigger the trigger you have chosen. Be sure to ensure that the trigger is simple to perform.

Without moving many muscles. Examples include the rubbing of your earlobes, rubbing your palms, or rubbing your fingers. The most important thing is to stop the trigger right away when positive emotions are at their highest.

4. Repeat - To get the most effective outcomes you should repeat the steps five times, taking a break between each attempt. Make sure to enjoy the exercise as much as you can to increase the positive feelings that are being held.

5. Keep a record if you've followed these steps properly, you'll be feeling the positive emotions that you've created every when you use the trigger. It is important to keep using the trigger to keep the brain from forgetting about the anchor.

Removal of self-doubt

Being critical of yourself is a sure indicator of low self-confidence and a negative mental attitude. The "inner critic" is an inner voice within each person who constantly reminds the person of their weaknesses and fears.

When it comes to brain training, having total control over your mind and maintaining a positive attitude is essential. To utilize Neuro-Linguistic Programming in achieving this just comply with these instructions:

1. Observe your inner voice. It must be one that you can actually hear inside your head. Are you hearing your own voice or another person's? What do you feel like when listening to the voice in your head?

2. Play around with the voice by manipulating it the duration you'd like. It is important to note that this mental practice is also beneficial for developing your language intelligence.

3. Take a break from the voice by adding static or moving it to distant locations as well as playing some music.

4. Then, convince that inner voice inside you to allow you to listen to it when it has something that is more effective.

After you've completed these two NLP techniques discussed in this chapter it's up to you whether or not you'd like to progress to more advanced NLP techniques.

There are a variety of professional groups offering Neuro-Linguistic Programming courses locally and online. Of course, many of them charge customers for their services. It is possible to find these businesses online if you are looking to go to the next level.

Chapter 8: What To Do To Enhance Memory Power

The memories we have are an important aspect of our identity. The unfortunate reality is that as we get older the quality of our memories decreases. As we get older, the loss of memory gets worse to the point where we may require to be looked after. A lot of us worry about that our memory is deteriorating, particularly when we are unable to remember where we last put the keys to our house or if we are unable to figure it out during an exam. Scientists have discovered the many ways our brains change and the ways in which their capacity may change and expand. There are many methods to improve the power of your memory.

Paying Attention

Attention is vital in the field of memory retention. To be able to recall things, i.e. to ensure that your information stored and transferred from short-term memory to the long-term memory, you have to be paying attentively to what's being discussed or instructed. This will allow you to keep the information that you will need to use in the future.

Make sure to eliminate all distractions that might affect your attention. Particularly especially for those who are students, it could be difficult to focus and focus when you are distracted. Make sure you be in a location which is free of television, music, or any other thing that could distract your attention from studying effectively.

Rephrase the information

If people learn or study new concepts, they keep the knowledge in a manner that they be able to comprehend it. When you try to describe something to someone else you are able to explain it and attempt to help them comprehend but you are unable to comprehend it for them. To enhance memory capacity, it is necessary to save the information they've learned in a manner that they are capable of understanding it.

If you're unsure about the concept behind a phrase, try to clarify the meaning in accordance with your knowledge. This will allow you remember the information you've learned and be able to comprehend the meaning behind it.

Discover New Things

Consider your mind as a bodybuilder whom you watch workout as they lift heavy weights. Bodybuilders are always working to strengthen their muscles while the greater they work weights, the more powerful they become. They don't stay with one weight , thinking that they'll get stronger. They test themselves by lifting various sizes of weight to get more powerful.

This is the same with your brain. The more you build your memory's muscle strength the more powerful it gets. Your brain will be always challenged and learning new skills. The new skills that you acquire will increase the memory power of your brain. This can be accomplished by learning a new instrument or language, and/or playing games of the mind.

Exercising

The benefits of exercise include cognitive advantages. It aids in the delivery of nutrients and oxygen to assist the body in creating new brain cells which will aid in memory storage. There are some simple exercises you can try improve your memory capacity. Meditation, walking, jogging and more. can help your body gain the memory storage capacity it needs.

Manage Mental Stresses

Stressors are experienced by people in their lives on a regular basis. The daily routines we engage in create mental tensions, like anxiety, stress and depression, among others. When you're under stress the body releases a hormone known as cortisol. This hormone is thought to hinder the brain's ability to remember things. The stress of mental life has profound effects on your mental behaviour and decrease the capacity to recall long-term memories whenever you require it.

It is possible to engage in exercise and other activities to alleviate depression, stress or anxiety. Socialize, discuss the issues you're experiencing with your trusted family or friends members, eliminate harmful traits or take part in physical activities.

Get enough rest

Sleep is essential to improve memory and learn. If you are able to rest enough increases the likelihood of being in a position to absorb new information, be able to retrieve it , and comprehend it. Insufficient sleep lowers levels of energy, making it hard to focus or concentrate on any subject. The memory of your brain also declines due to the absence of sleep, which is what your body needs. Sleep can help you retain information better and process information faster.

You must adhere the same schedule for your sleeping. Sleep in the same hour each night , and rise to the same hour each morning. Be careful not to disrupt your sleep pattern as it could disrupt your sleep routine.

Activity 1

Simple game that can help improve memory Remember 10 random items.

Choose 10 random items and then list them. You can time yourself, perhaps you will need to start with a longer time period, and then decrease the time after you repeat the procedure. In the allotted time you should try to recall the 10 things you need to remember.

You can either (a) make an entire story that includes each of the 10 items or (b) link with the items using similarity or another type of relationship.

For instance, here are just a few examples such as a fork, paper clip the clock ... ... and so on.

(a) (a) I dropped an object on the ground and then was bent to retrieve it, and I saw a paper clip close to it. Then, I heard the clock chime 2 o'clock. I'm running in the middle of an afternoon course!

(b) Imagine this: Use the fork to grasp an old newspaper clip...

Activity 2

Deep breathing and meditation can help alleviate stress that could cause memory loss. Think of happy times and you will find yourself smiling to let go of those moments of worry and stress. A positive mind can remember better.

Improved Concentration

To be able to retain information it is essential to be able to focus on what they're learning or hearing, seeing or reading, or just doing something. A lot of people have difficulty to complete an assignment because of a lack of focus. There are numerous methods that people can employ to increase their concentration.

What is Concentration?

Concentration is the process by which your mind - with all means and efforts is trying to direct your attention to a particular thing you're studying or listening to in the times. Many people mistake concentration and attention span. Attention span refers to being in a position to focus on something for a long time or time.

An inability to concentrate could be caused by a range of reasons. It could be due to the fact that many people struggle with not being able to focus on any distractions or interruptions. Age is also the cause of a decrease in concentration, brain injuries, mental healthissues, poor sleep, and so on. could also be factors that impact our concentration.

A lot of people who aren't able to or do not have capacity to focus regularly would like to be able to. When they are frustrated by trying to be more focused it can lead to anxiety, which can affect your concentration more. There are steps you can follow to give your brain the boost it requires to focus its attention on a specific task and thus be able to concentrate more effectively.

Visit Nature

If you're being in one place all the time, whether doing work or watching TV, it gets exhausting. Being in nature isn't an ideal thing to do. The natural environment has been shown to have positive effects on brains and people. Plants around the office has been suggested that it can help people focus and may even increase productivity.

The natural and green environments, can be an effective method to improve productivity and brain development. If you're looking to improve your focus, then eating lunch outside in the garden is a good idea. A walk in the garden for 20 minutes each day is a great way to boost your memory. The addition of plants to your workplace or even in your home is another option which can yield positive outcomes. Try it!

A Pause

The things that happen in your environment can make you feel overwhelmed particularly when you are in the group of people who tend to be easily distracted or not able to focus on the background noise. A break might appear like something that should not be considered, particularly when you're faced with many tasks that are piled up in front of you however, evidence has proved that having a break can dramatically increase your capacity to focus.

Take care of yourself

We've all experienced those times where we are overwhelmed by all the things we do and then it seems like your brain isn't fully absorbing everything that it has to absorb. That's when you should take a break, grab an iced beverage, have a bite of fruit or snack, or take short walks in the sun.

The body needs to be reenergized to help you get to the end of your day. In lieu of placing your head under pressure to get your work done, nourish your body by eating well and incorporating a little physical exercise.

Schedule emailing time

There are times when people don't know when to stop checking their email. People who constantly switch between email and work activities, have difficulty to concentrate on a single job. Breaking from emailing is an option. Set a time when you'll need to login to email to help you focus on one task at one time.

Stop Cell Notifications, and Social Media

It could be text messages or phone calls which come in, or even social media notifications - all of these things can be enough to distract you from the things you're trying to concentrate on. Social media is extremely distracting since we are focused on others instead of being productive. Although the notifications are only brief that sound like tiny vibrations or pings, they are enough to cause your brain into a state of disorientation.

Switching off your mobile is one method that you can employ to be productive. Also, consider turning it to silent. Beware of the urge to engage in social media because it could affect the performance of your work.

Change Your Environment

A workplace's environment plays an important impact on how well we are capable of staying productive in our work and focus. A messy workplace will usually slow productivity and cause your mind to feel as if everything is out of all over the.

For better concentration, try making some changes to your workplace or your place of work. If you tend to study in your bedroom, set up your own work space that can solely be used for doing your work. Make sure your desk is tidy to keep it neat. Create your workspace in accordance with the colors and objects you love.

Listen to music

Some people might think that music could be distracting, however it actually helps increase concentration. Music playing softly on the background can ease your mind and soothe the atmosphere in your workplace. In doing so it is crucial to select the music you like best because songs you like or dislike could result in distractions.

Select music that is classical or natural since they've been shown to keep people focused. Be sure the volume is kept low and the music is quiet so as not to distract you.

Evaluate Your Diet

In the next chapter (chapter 9) We will concentrate on foods that boost your memory. Foods can affect cognitive functions. Thus, it is important to be mindful of the food they consume as they can affect the ability to concentrate and memory. Eliminating foods that have high levels of sugar, fatty foods , and ones which are oily is a good first step. Instead, concentrate on food items which will improve your ability to concentrate and remember. That means eating a balanced diet and being aware of the foods you put in your body will impact the efficiency of your brain.

Activity 1

Choose from the above list of small adjustments to integrate into your routine. Check in and make adjustments as necessary. Don't overload yourself with too many changes all at one time. Begin with a small step every time.

Activity 2

Take a moment to unwind from work or studying. Relax and breathe deeply to calm your body and mind. Relaxed people can focus better. If you're relaxed, you'll be able to accomplish more.

Memorizing

When we remember information and attempt to store the information into our short-term memory. This is when we are able to remember a constant intake of information, which is then associated with the neurons. They get stronger and stronger which causes the brain to expend less energy to keep track of things. This helps to improve memory.

The brain's structure changes as we learn and start to store information. Many people consider memorizing not essential and prefer to practice critical thinking abilities. What they don't know is that keeping the information they've acquired is what allows them to think in a critical manner.

Learning to memorize helps train your brain to retain information. Your brain is bolstered through the activities you engage in. It helps you to remember and store any other information you come across. Instead of cramming - - which is often confused with memorizing - it can aid your brain in becoming more attentive to the knowledge it has saved. This is why students can retain that periodic table and multiplication tables, and the sounds each alphabet produces as well as other sounds. Because they were taught to remember all the fundamental knowledge facts and details.

The benefits of memorizing are numerous and instead of dismissing it, you should read more to find the positive aspect of it.

Improves Understanding

Learning relevant facts or information in manners that are beneficial for the reader or learner is a way to increase their capacity to comprehend. Also, it improves the brain's capacity to absorb new information.

Enhances Memory

When you learn your information, your memory increases throughout the entire process. The brain's function grows in size and is enhanced, as do any related structures to memory in the brain. The brain's flexibility increases, which is known as neural plasticity.

Enhances Creativity

When your brain becomes enthralled to content, the space within the brain's circuitry can facilitate the brain to think more creatively. Also, when you are able to memorize your brain's content, what it does is to force you to pay focus to the content you are learning, which increases your capacity to focus.

Activity 1

To increase your ability to recall information, engage in something like fixing the order in which things are done. For instance, ask someone else tell you three things that they did in the past and then repeat the information in the same order.

Activity 2

Try to remember the multiplication tables. It is possible to alter it to reverse tables of multiplication in division terms. For instance, 7 8 = 56 can be remembered as 56 / 7 = 8, and 56 / 8 = 7.

You must continue to work on your memory to learn the square numbers 2 + 2 = 4 3 + 3 = 9. 4 x 4 = 16 ... ... 10. 10-x10 = 100. 11 eleven times 11 equals 121. 12 + 12 = 144.

Activity 3

Don't get angry at yourself when you discover that you are unable to remember the information. Take your time and breathe deeply before you attempt at memorizing the information.

Improving Short-term Memory

It can be very depressing when you are unable to remember the name of someone, just only a few minutes after having learned it. You may not remember anything that you've learned three minutes ago. This is known as short-term memory loss. It is defined as the time being unable to remember the things you've done, seen and planned to do, or even heard recently. It's a normal part of growing older, but it can be difficult. It could also indicate that we're about to be tired, and that it could be a sign of a more serious issue for instance mental health problems or a brain injury, as well as dementia.

What is short-term memory?

It's where your brain receives the little amount of information just absorbed, and store it. It's an additional stage of multi-stored memory . It is split between short-term memory and working memory. The short-term memory is seven things can be saved at any one time. The amount of time you can store information is restricted, because when data is stored it could be lost due to interruptions or as the time passes through. The information is encoded once audio information is converted into visual.

When we talk about the loss of short-term memory We are talking about recently acquired information that is lost. The majority of people end up unaware of the reason they went into a space and where they put their keys, or forgetting the breakfast they had and asking the same questions repeatedly or even forgetting a book they've just read.

There's a method that determines whether you suffer from temporary memory impairment. If you see a doctor and they'll guide you through a set of questions and exercises to determine the severity of the loss of memory. The doctor will inquire about any recent injuries as well as your general life and health, the medications you take, your emotional state sleep patterns, and drinking habits. The next step is looking to see if there are any medical conditions, taking blood tests to test for other illnesses that can aid in identifying your symptoms. Your doctor may also have to conduct brain scansto to test your ability to concentrate and ask you questions that are basic like the date and your name, as well as make a few letters or even speak with you about recent eventsto establish the reason for the problem.

Reasons for short-term memory loss

There are a variety of possible causes for temporary memory impairment. It could be due to the process of ageing, brain tumors bleeding within your brain , concussions, blood clots, and other injuries to the brain. Brain infections or the brain, mental health issues, stress and substance abuse disorders. sleeping insufficiently, taking certain medications such as Post-traumatic Stress Disorder (PTSD) and many more.

In certain instances the loss of short-term memory may not be a problem however that doesn't mean it shouldn't be avoided. Certain reasons for short-term memory loss could worsen over time, and threaten the loss of your memory over time. In addition to treatments, there are home strategies you can engage in and change your habits to increase you short-term memory.

Make a list of things to do.

We all find ourselves at the moment that we head to the supermarket to purchase a particular item. We go to the store, look for other products to purchase, and then shop then, by the time we return home, the main item we came to the store looking to purchase in the first place and the most significant one of all, is gone. This happens to the best of us. When this occurs, we get angry.

To avoid this, you can create an agenda of things to do or items to buy to assist you in buying the items you require which you may have overlooked trying to remember them in your head. This will allow you to stay on the right track and lower the likelihood of becoming overwhelmed.

Make use of Creative and unusual fonts

Our eyes are frequently intrigued and drawn by anything that is unique. Your eyes will get used to being exposed to the same thing day after day. It requires a lot of focus when you apply your attention to something, and it's not an ideal idea to change your fonts often. This will make it simpler for your mind to recall what you read or experienced.

Doodling

Many people are annoyed when they see others drawing on paper, particularly teachers. Doodling can inspire individuals to develop imaginative ways of thinking, and also to develop new ideas. To rapidly recall concepts and retrieving information. If you start to draw on paper, your brain begins to think, remember and generate innovative concepts.

Do your best to maintain a good posture

Studies have proven that a healthy posture can boost memory and create an energy boost. If you start slouching, and your eyes begin to look drowsy it is likely that you will recall memories that are negative. Sitting up is when blood flow is increased and you're likely to remember positive memories and not negative ones.

Maintain a Healthy Diet

The right type of foods is an essential element of maintaining a healthy memory. When you have a balanced diet cognitive function as well as memory improves. A diet that is rich in fruits, vegetables, and omega 3's will keep your memory intact as you get older. Foods can impact the brain's capacity to function and keep memory. Choose healthy, nutritious foods that include full of whole grains vegetables, fruits, and healthy meats.

Chewing Gum

The idea of chewing gum during learning may sound odd however, in actual studies have proven that chewing gum can improve the accuracy of learning. A brain region called the hippocampus, which is responsible which is responsible for memory, has increased activity.

Activity 1

Regular exercise can help enhance the short-term memory of your. Every day, do cardio prior to starting your day. If cardio isn't your thing or something you enjoy include yoga in your routine of exercise.

Activity 2

Make a memory card game match game. Set up a collection of pictures or symbols or even word cards. Make sure the exact objects are copied. Shuffle and put the cards on top. Begin by opening 2 cards at a go, trying to match them to the identical pair. Repeat the game. This game trains our minds to instantly recall the last time we saw that particular card image, symbol or word. It could also be a multi-player game to test your brain's ability and beat the opponent(s).

Activity 3

Make a plan for your day or work schedule using checklists to aid in organizing your short-term recollection of what needs to be accomplished or things you need to keep in mind.

Examples include:

* Shopping list for groceries

* Birthdates and other events

* Project scheduling

* To-do-list

Improving Long-term Memory

The memories that you have will begin to decay even before they've begun to develop. It is impossible to count all the memories we've had and if we could we'd realize that the majority of our memories aren't readily accessible. Not just what happened at the beginning of the day. In the course of our lives and the experiences we have every day people are able to build lasting memories. However, how do we take care of them and aid our brain in keeping the memories?

What is Long-term Memory?

Long-term memory is the kind of memories that are more lasting. The brain stores data over a lengthy duration of. That means your brain is capable of recalling details, the way to finish tasks, and recall your way to home. Being able to recall the events of last night, 20 years ago or even just five hours ago, indicates that it's a long-lasting memory.

What happens to memory when it changes from short-term into long-term memory is through the hippocampus. The information is processed there before being decoded various sensory regions of the cortex. It is connected with the hippocampus. It then redirects the different sensory areas back to their source. All information is organized according to their proper places. And when you wish to revisit an experience the information is transferred to the hippocampus once more.

One of the things that is known about long-term memory is that it is dependent on the length of time a memory will persist in accordance with the way it was stored in the mind. In the event that you knew of an event and the memory is vivid, it remains vivid. The long-term memories are often without conscious thought and not all are the same. While some can be quickly brought into your the mind, others require numerous signals to get them to focus, as they've been weakened. Memory that is frequently accessible in the brain are those that get stronger. The long-term memory can last for between weeks and the length of several years.

Different types of long-term memory

1. Implicit Memories

These memories are are not conscious. This includes procedural memory meaning that the memories are defined by the movements of your body. It could be about how to prepare a certain dessert, driving or operate computers.

2. Explicit Memories

They are the memories that are accessible within the consciousness. They are usually referred to as declarative memories. They are split into two types of memories:

1.) A semantic memory is what you are aware of about the world and

2.) Memory that is episodic of specific events.

As time passes as time passes, memories of the long term change. Information will be stored in the short-term memory and then certain portions will be transferred into longer-term memories. The brain works as a computer and store data on the hard disks in computers. When you need the information, it will be retrieved from the long-term storage due to the signals within your environment. The long-term memory of each individual will not remain the same as they're altered with time. Every time a memory is stored, it's recoded by other neurons, resulting in a different version from the original.

What causes long-term memory loss?

Similar to temporary memory impairment, the loss of long-term memory can be caused by a variety of reasons. It can be due to mental health issues, like depression or stress as well as the side effects of prescription medications, B-12 deficiency or excess fluid in the brain, which could be reversed. Long-term memory loss is typically caused by brain damage and cannot be reversed easily. The improvement can be triggered by the severity of the damage and the areas of the brain that are affected. Alcohol and drugs may cause memory loss for a long time and a concussion that is an extremely serious brain injury also can result in memory loss. A serious brain cancer, brain inflammation or epilepsy, loss of oxygen with severe seizures, and strokes, too.

It is essential to increase your memory over time to improve your long-term memory, and you can do this by making use of your memories to ensure they are able to last longer. People who have suffered from memory loss over the long term are unable to remembering important information However, you can overcome this by following these steps.

Access Memories Every now and then

The more information you can store within the brain and the more you recall them, the stronger they become more powerful. The reason is that the prefrontal cortex and the silent engrams are developed within a few weeks. Recalling and reminiscing can help to strengthen the process as well.

Journaling

Note-taking has proved to be among the most effective methods to consolidate information and information in your long-term memory. By having every detail and detail written down, you'll recall memorable experiences, milestones and relationships, etc. Journaling can assist in recalling that specific time in the future.

Take Care of Your Mental Health

Depression, stress and anxiety are the most common reasons for memory problems. These mental disorders can affect the brain's processing ability and ability to focus. The majority of people aren't aware of the time they go through a depression, or if they're overwhelmed or even anxious. The need to seek medical treatment if you begin to feel like you are falling is a crucial element of maintaining your health and taking good care of your mental wellbeing.

Quiz Yourself

Testing yourself regularly is a great method to improve your memory. Test your brain with an exam, as it shows you're learning. It is possible to assess your knowledge, identify the strengths as well as weaknesses, and be able to improve these. This can help you remember what you've learned and discover what your brain has kept.

Making use of Smartphones the right Way

Technology has evolved into an exciting and continuous aspect of our life. It has made it simpler to get information, and keep it in a safe place. But if you misuse it, it won't benefit you. Be confident in the possibility that these phones come with alarms and reminders, and the ability to take notes instead of continually trying everything on your mind. The clutter of your brain with numerous reminders isn't effective for your brain's performance. Also, try to capture pictures of the experiences you experience to ensure that your mind retains information in your long-term memory.

Activity 1

Try a game that involves making a list of the most commonly used fundamental knowledge and facts to enhance your memory for the long run. For instance, you can you can ask yourself questions like:

Who was the first to walk on the moon?

Who was the person who invented electricity?

What symbols appear in your country's bank notes?

In this way, this exercise can help you improve your memory.

Activity 2

Begin to make a habit of journal writing. Write down small and large occasions using descriptive emotions. This will assist you in keep a record of past events for the near future.

3rd Activity

Take a listen to classical, instrumental or soft music to discover how to take a break from the stress of your hectic schedule on a regular basis. Be mindful of your mental well-being.

Brain Exercises to Improve Memory Memory

Exercise is among the most vital methods of ensuring your body is healthy. You may know when it is time to work out and the reasons behind it but did you realize that your mind requires exercise to keep it alert and strong to keep your memory intact? In addition to the physical condition, the same is true for the health of your brain and that is something that must be maintained to reduce the chance of developing diseases and other health problems which are a result of age.

Regular exercise and a healthy lifestyle can help keep your memory and mind strong. Include brain exercises in your routine to keep your brain sharp and sharp.

Mentally Performing Math

When we face an Math issue to solve and we rush for help from our trusted calculator or require the assistance of paper and pencil. In lieu of reaching out for the tools to aid you in solving Math problems, begin by tackling easy Math problems inside your mind.

The best way to take care of your body is taking care of Your Mind

It is important to recognize that it is important to take good care of your body to take good care of the mind. Exercise can help many parts of the body to make them more efficient, which includes your brain. It shields the brain from shrinking as we age, and may make you more intelligent. It also enhances the development of new brain cells within the hippocampus in the brain, which is responsible for memory.

A better mind starts with exercise.

Reduce multitasking

Multitasking is a great option to complete various tasks at once. Although it can be beneficial for the moment, it's best not to create the norm. The thing that many do not know is that multitasking can distract your mind and cause confusion over what it's working on and how it should actually be doing.

Be aware of what you're doing at the moment. When you store things that you don't want to keep, tell yourself about the place you placed the item, so that your brain has the ability to recall the information later.

Improve Your Vocabulary

Sometimes, we hear people using large and new terms that we usually don't understand. Although learning a new term will increase your vocabulary and help you appear smarter however, it also becomes an instruction in vocabulary that will stimulate your brain. There are many brain regions including auditory and visual processing, are involved in the words and phrases.

The simple process of expanding your vocabulary could turn into a thrilling game of a vocabulary class that can boost your mind.

By Using the Five Senses

If you are using all of your senses, it is providing your brain with a required workout.

Instead of performing tasks that only use the one of your senses focus, consider using all five. This will strengthen your brain as well as increase the intensity of all your senses. Go to a new place and pay attention to the sensations of tasting, touching and hearing all simultaneously.

Create a Map using Memory

Anyone who has been taking the same route to work every day for over 5 years may believe that they know how to navigate the streets even if they close their eyes. This is until they have to guide others and experience trouble remembering the exact route. To test this idea, challenge your brain by making a map of your route you follow and writing down the street names in your memory. Once you've finished check your map against the actual map of the area or route.

To increase the difficulty and challenge To increase the difficulty, try recalling your entire neighborhood , or any other location you frequently visit. or any other location you'd like to visit.

Jigsaw Puzzles

Games such as jigsaw puzzles assist in numerous ways to boost your memory. When you play the game your eyes are focused on different pieces. You need to determine where each piece fits into the bigger picture. This is a fantastic method to test and work your brain. This is a motor skill that will improve the hand-eye coordination of your child, and develop various cognitive capacities and endurance. It's also a protective factor against cognitive decline due to visuospatial.

Activity 1

While reading take a notepad near by where you will be in a position to write down words you aren't sure about. Create a game in which you discover the meaning behind each word.

Activity 2

Play puzzles with jigsaws. You can plan a predetermined period of time in the day to finish a piece or a piece of puzzle. You can increase the number of pieces in the subsequent jigsaw puzzles as you get better. Enjoy!

This is the Natural Way to Boost Memory

In the fast-paced, modern world we live in, it's easy to lose track of the things we have to do and need to complete. We get overwhelmed that we lose focus and drift off tasks. Instead of seeking out items that marketers claim can help enhance memory there are plenty of methods to incorporate into your daily routine to boost your memory naturally. This will reduce the risk of developing age-related illnesses such as dementia and Alzheimer's disease. ensure that your mind stays active as you age.

Maintain an appropriate weight

As we have discussed in earlier chapters, when you work out physically, you also exercising your mind. This is why keeping the right weight for your body is vital for your health and keeping your mind and body in good health. Stay within the boundaries of your BMI because weight gain is among the causes of cognitive decline.

Obesity can alter how memory genes function in the brain. It may cause insulin resistance and inflammation that can negatively affect memory and the brain. It is also linked to the possibility of developing Alzheimer's Disease, which causes cognitive impairment and memory.

Staying Hydrated

To ensure that your brain and body to continue functioning in the correct way, it must be well-hydrated. If you don't have enough fluids in your body, the mind can be in a state of confusion, imaginings, as well as false appetite. Take plenty of fluids every daily, such as soups made from homemade smoothies, broths, water, non-caffeinated teas, non-sweetened vegetable juices, etc. In order to lessen the dangers of dehydration.

Socialize

Social interactions with others can boost your cognitive capabilities. You are less at chance of developing Alzheimer's disease and degenerative diseases. If you are social, many areas of your brain are active and the activities you participate in can benefit your brain.

If you're having a hard socializing with others or if you're an introvert, you should sign up for volunteer opportunities in your local area or join a group to remain in contact and in contact with your family and friends, playing games on the cards or attending seminars. Participating in activities that permit your brain to exercise is a skill for interaction that is involving other people and could be beneficial for your brain's short-term as well as long-term memory.

Omega-3 Fatty Acids

The body requires Omega-3-rich fatty acids can be one which can help in the development of your mind's cognitive function. They are found in supplements and are naturally found in fish, nuts and flaxseed. This healthy fat combats inflammation and slows the decline in cognitive capacity. (more information is in chapter 9)

Check the level of Vitamin D in your body.

Vitamin D is among the most vital nutrients your body needs , and it plays a crucial function. If you have low levels of vitamin D levels in your body, you could be at risk for problems with your health and a decline in cognitive performance. If your levels of vitamin D in your blood are lower than 20 nanograms/ml and you are experiencing an impairment in cognitive and memory abilities more quickly than those with normal levels of vitamin D. Therefore, you're at an increased chance of getting dementia. It is essential to visit your doctor and discuss taking a blood test to determine the need for vitamin D supplements.

Activity 1

Be sure to establish an effective routine of exercise to maintain a healthy weight. Be sure to eat an energizing diet that includes Omega 3 fatty acid. Do not forget to drink eight glasses of fluids per day.

Activity 2

Participate in activities that enable you to interact with others. The social setting will improve your mood, and , at the same providing your brain with the stimulation it needs. In your interactions with your old and new friends, take note of their conversations and learn more about them. This will help increase your concentration and focus (chapter 2) as well as acquire a vocabulary (chapter 6, chapter 6).).

A social gathering planned with a sporting event would have put the activities 1 and 2. You can kill the two birds that strike! Make it your own and have fun!

Simple Strategies to Improve Memory

Our brains have the capacity to store information in a vast memory. The issue is the moment we must recall or retrieve information from our memory. This is what is causing a lot of people to be frustrated. Being able to recall particular dates, dates, and even details whenever you need to is something everyone wants to achieve however it can be difficult.

Particularly in a time when information is readily available every minute and is readily available. In this day and age we are so accustomed to the abundance of information available so that whenever we're looking for something new we instantly go to the internet, not our minds. This can cause a decline in the brain's functions. However, there are a few simple techniques that can improve memory.

Utilize Visual Imagery

Visual cues are generally easier to recall than words. Making images of what you'll need to remember will aid in your memory. Your mind can create symbols that are associated with the knowledge you've absorbed as a significant portion the memory you have is visually. Connecting words to images helps you to recall and hold the information you've learned.

Know the Information

If you read new information and gain knowledge through it, the brain is working to comprehend what you are studying. In the event that the material is simple to comprehend and makes sense it is easier to remember. If you are unable to comprehend what you are reading, then your mind will have a difficult remembering the facts. If you find the information you're reading hard to comprehend, you should spend more time understanding the subject before you attempt to recall the details.

Dozing off after studying

The brain process and store the information you've learned in the course of your are asleep. Before you fall asleep go over the information you've learned for the time you require, and then fall asleep and during sleep, the knowledge is stored in your brain.

Grouping Information

If you are looking to remember details, you should create meaningful groups to simplify the information to be able to comprehend. For instance, if you are trying to remember some cartoon names, simply abbreviate the initial letters of each name, so that you will be in a position to link the data. If the abbreviation can be associated with an image it is simpler to visualize the image and then remember the words.

Rhyming

Rhymes are a form of memory that help you learn. The process of collecting your information and making rhymes from the material you're learning will increase the recall of information significantly.

Activity 1

Create visual images that help you remember what you've learned or to make a an outline of words or a sequence of steps for doing something. If we must purchase five things from the store such as bread, watermelon, broccoli as well as cooking oil, peanuts and watermelon. Imagine yourself sitting on the head of a watermelon with earrings made of broccoli eating peanuts, while you accidentally spill cooking oil onto the bread! The more funny and absurd images you can imagine, is, the easier it will be to remember the information.

Activity 2

Transform your learning material into fun songs or rhymes, which will help you remember the information. Music is believed to help you improve your memory. It's also a good method to relieve stress. It can also be an enjoyable moment in recalling your studies documents.

Foods that improve memory

In earlier chapters, we've discussed the importance of exercise and keeping your weight in check to increase memory. While exercise is essential however, it's not enough without eating healthy food. Did you ever hear the phrase "you have what you consume?" What you eat is the primary factor that determines whether you'll perform certain activities.

Food is a vital part of living and there are a variety of kinds of food options to pick from. In the final analysis what you put into your body is important, as the food we consume has an enormous impact on the structure and health of our brains.

The brain consumes 20 percent of your body's calories because it is a highly energy-intensive organ. It requires plenty of energy to maintain focused throughout the day. Also, it requires certain nutrients to be healthy. Foods that are healthy and a balanced diet can help sharpen your the focus of your mind, increasing memory improving the amount of time you spend on your mind and your brain functioning.

As we age and get older, it is evident that our body, which includes your brain , ages with us. However, the good news is that you can boost your memory by maintaining an active lifestyle. Consume a wide range of well-curated foods. Here is a list of dishes which will do what you need!

Fatty Fish

* Trout

* Salmon

* Sardines

* Herring

* Cod

* Can of Light Tuna

* Pollack

* Kippers

* Mackerel

These fish with fatty content are an excellent source of food for consumption because they're loaded with omega-3 fatty acids that are vital to improve memory. They help improve the brain structure of neurons, which are brain cells. Omega-3 reduces the risk of mental decline , and reduces the risk of developing Alzheimer's disease.

Insufficient omega-3 intake can cause brain damage as well as depression. Fish consumption has beneficial health effects, particularly for the brain. If you are unable to take fish as a food, talk to your doctor to see the possibility of being given omega-3 supplements.

Leafy and green vegetables

* Kale

* Broccoli

* Spinach

* Collards

* Turnips

* Cabbage

* Cauliflower

* Bok Choy

* Brussel Sprouts

These vegetables are loaded with nutrients that can help support brain health and help protect against damage to the brain. They are rich in antioxidants including glucosinolates and glucosinolates flavonoids, folate, vitamin K lutein beta carotene, and minerals.

They slow down cognitive decline They also produce isothiocyanates, which lower the oxidative stress, and reduce the risk of developing neurodegenerative disorders.

Berries

* Blackberries

* Blackcurrants

* Mulberries

* Blueberries

* Strawberries

Flavonoids present in berries, aid in slowing memory loss and short-term memory loss. They also contain antioxidants that help reduce inflammation and the stress of oxidative. Berries lower inflammation across the body, and help brain cells to create new connections, and boost memory and learning. They also improve the connections among brain cells.

Tea and Coffee

Get your day started with a cup or tea. These beverages offer more than just an increase in your short-term memory they also aid in forming new memories. The caffeine content in coffee and tea help boost alertness, by blocking the chemical messenger that makes you sleepy. Your mood will be brighter and improve throughout the day . It will improve focus, which is helpful in completing those things that need to be completed.

Particularly coffee, can reduce the risk of developing neurological diseases like Parkinson's disease and Alzheimer's. This includes cognitive decline and stroke. Be aware of what amount of sugar that you are including in your tea and coffee.

Whole Grains

* Brown rice

* Oatmeal

* Whole-grain bread

* Whole-grain pasta

* Bulgur wheat

167

* Barley

These are excellent foods to consume if you wish to get more benefits from Vitamin E. They can provide you with energy and are essential for your body to maintain the focus. Wholegrains that are low in GI are the most beneficial since they slowly release energy into the bloodstream, bringing you energy. Wholegrains help reduce mental fog and irritation.

Nuts and seeds

* Pumpkin seeds

* Peanuts

* Walnuts

* Cashews

* Almonds

* Flaxseed

* Chia seeds

* Brazil nuts

Seeds and nuts contain proteins and unsaturated fats to help boost energy levels.

They help keep your brain healthy and contain nutrients that protect against inflammation, cancer and neurological illnesses.

The unsaturated fats that are found in some seeds as well as nuts can help lower blood pressure as well as blood pressure. They aid in brain health, have powerful antioxidants, and are particularly beneficial in pumpkin seeds, which shield both the brain and body from the effects of radical damage.

Other food items you can enjoy that aid in improving memory are:

* Eggs

* Dark chocolate

* Avocados

* Tomatoes

* Turmeric

* Sage

* Soy products

Nutrients

Other essential nutrients for brain healthand are is essential to neural signaling, learning and memory, which reduces brain fog and impair brain function. Other nutrients that aid with the control of nerve signals:

* Iron

* Magnesium

* Copper

* Zinc

Activity 1

Make use of the lists above of various types of food items to make your weekly menu. Take a small amount of each different types of food. Make it as you will enjoy the brain- and memory-based food.

Games to Enhance Memory

We play games not just for fun however, they also help improve memory, something the majority of people aren't aware of. As with the human body the brain requires frequent workouts to ensure it is performing its best functioning. Training your brain can improve how it reacts, improve its ability to think and help keep it sharp.

Give a few minutes in your time each day to these games to enhance your brain.

* Crossword Puzzles The games test your vocabulary, and draw inspiration from popular culture, history and science.

* Sudoku - Depends upon short-term memory. It stimulates brain regions and helps with memory in order to learn numbers and apply the ability to think logically to place numbers in the correct grid.

* Jigsaw Puzzles - This game utilizes both the right and left side of your brain all simultaneously. It increases speed, and spatial thinking, as your brain is working to recognize the pieces and how they belong.

* Chess is among the most well-known games, and is now the standard for anyone looking for something intellectually difficult. It's all about studying the board and planning the next step. It requires both long and short-term memory, which will house the strategies you have crafted.

* Rebus Puzzles - This game has some excellent questions that have clues within them that have to be deduced. It boosts brain and memory capacity; tests your knowledge of cliches and phrases.

* Concentration The game has evolved into a variety of forms, that aid children in improving their the ability to concentrate and retain information. It's all about knowing which card the next match is, and also where you last observed. The ball's location inside the cup could be depending on the magician's constant changing their positions.

Other games that you could play to stimulate your brain, boost concentration and even assist with multitasking include: Clevermind, Lumosity, Braingle, Happy Neuron Elevate, Broken phone and numerous others.

Activity 1

How does stress affect your Brain?

Are you stressed and unable to focus? Is your brain fried? Are you struggling to keep your focus and complete tasks? This could be the case, not just a catchy slogan. Stress can cause grave damage, including impairment of mental health, mood and cognition.

Stress is a common and necessary part of our day (there are good stress and bad, but it's certainly not all awful). What people are saying and doing, the way people respond to your actions and words the information you receive in the mail or through email -- you have take control of these events. They'll occur, which is why stress can be a factor.

Stress can result in an rise in cortisol. Cortisol, in layman's sense, is similar to rust in the brain. The most serious issue is that Alzheimer's disease is associated with stress, which is why this is so serious! Stress can cause shrinkage of the area of the hippocampus (memory) and cause damage to neurons.

The message is clear The key is to reduce stress levels. is essential to maintaining your mental well-being, and in many ways. It's a task that's much easier to accomplish than it is said to be.

Note: In subsequent chapters I will discuss the effects of stress on your brain while trying to learn, and why getting rid of stress quickly is vital.

How can you lessen stress for yourself?

Here are some suggestions on how to alleviate the stress that can affect your life.

Join the gym

Training for resistance is a fantastic way to boost the flow of oxygen to the brain, while reducing stress. Avoid working out in excess, as excessive exercise isn't good for you. I suggest doing 2-5 workouts per week, based on your goals as well as your nutrition. For people who are not athletes 3 times per week is ideal. It should take about 30 to 45 minutes to complete a full body exercise.

* Cardio, however my preferred method is intervals. You can go very fast or increasing intensity for a shorter duration, and then return to the same pace but with a more relaxed pace to rest. There's no reason that for cardio to last longer than 15 minutes, unless of course you suffer from a heart problem and then you should you should opt for a longer steady state cardio.

Meditation

I'm pretty sure that I'm losing a few of readers in this particular post. The first time I heard of meditation, I thought, "Yeah, that's not for me." The idea of sitting still and trying not to think for five, ten 15 or 60 minutes sounded like a nightmare and, in some cases, impossible. That's until I discovered Binaural Beats that made the experience almost too simple. To find out more, go here.

Meditation can help improve concentration and allow us to think effectively in stressful situations in the moments that matter the most. MRI scans of individuals who have sat in meditation for long periods of time have demonstrated more activity in brain regions involved when paying close attention. If disturbing sound effects were played to a group of people who were taking the MRI examination, it was found the sound did not have a significant impact on the brain regions that are involved in decision-making and emotion when compared to those who did not meditate or those who are less experienced in meditating. The researchers have found that meditation can alter your DNA! According to an Harvard study conducted after 30 days of meditation the participants altered up to 500 pieces of their DNA

"By the analysis of samples from blood, the researchers discovered that 2209 genes differed in expressed (switched between off and on) between long-term meditators and the control group. Particularly, 1275 genes are up-regulated (their activity increased) as well as 934 that were down-regulated (their activity decreased). The study also revealed the expression of 1561 genes in a different way between those who completed the eight weeks of meditation and the group that was a control. In particular, 874 genes were up-regulated, while 687 genes were downregulated. Also that meditation, whether in the long or short term triggers thousands of genes switch up or down." 2

Less Television

* It is recommended to limit your time spent watching television to less than an hour each day. It's difficult to convince however, continue going.

People enjoy sitting watching television or turning into zombies, simply trance-like for long periods of time! The problem is that television doesn't exhaust your brain's capacity or let it recharge. Aren't you tired after a couple of hours of television? The eyes have become swollen and exhausted because you've been glued to the boob for so long. Nobody has become more intelligent, wealthier or had more energy become more fit after watching television for hours each day. Another important thing to remember is that most people are in low-level hypnosis while watching television. I am curious about the effect that the hours of TV you watch can have on your mind every month? The only thing I can tell you is this Garbage in equals garbage out.

Gratitude Journal

One of the best ways to start or finish your day is to use an appreciation journal. Every day or night note down your reasons for being happy about, what you looking forward to and what you plan to do in the coming days or hours to become an improved version of yourself and more. It can help keep you optimistic and encouraged. Journals of gratitude are a wonderful method to remind yourself how great you are even when you feel like you're not.

Deep Breathing

"Deep breathing" or oxygen load. Deep breathing increases the levels of oxygen and cerebral blood circulation. A few minutes of deep breathing every day can make a big impact on the quality of your life as well as the functioning of your brain, and also provide oxygen into the brain. One technique I learnt from Tony Robbins is the 1:4-to-2 method. For each second you breathe in take your breath in at four times the length then exhale for the same time that you breathed. If you can breathe by putting your mouth in for five seconds, then hold the breath for 20 minutes, and then breathe out for 10 seconds. Do this once. Repeat for 10 minutes and then tell me that you're more calm, less stressed, and full of energy. The first time I tried it, it was like I had drank a cup of coffee! As with most of us, I breathed shallowly frequently.

Yoga

* I am a fan of watching my evening yoga DVD with my friend just before getting ready for

bed (never imagined I'd write about that). It helps me get rid of all my tension and leaves me at ease and ready for sleep. The stretching, as well as concentrated deep breathing, takes all stress from me.

What programs or services do I recommend to ease stress?

Binaural Beats Binaural Beats (a mind development tool)

I have a variety of systems:

1) Omharmonics

2.) Holosync

3) Brain evolution

4) Unlimited IQ

I love to switch them around because it is true that variation is the best spice in life! Each comes with a variety of optionsfor focusing wake up, sleeping and waking up, better meditation, creative and calming down.

Massage

There are numerous benefits to massage like relaxation, better sleep, increased health, better recovery from exercise, and the list could go on and on. If you're looking to shed fat and strengthen your muscles, this can aid in recovering from your workout faster and with greater efficiency.

Acupuncture

There are numerous benefits to Acupuncture, which are comparable to massage, for instance the ability to reduce stress, boost the quality of your life, and improve your sleep. By improving any one or more of the above areas can make it much easier to reach your goals.

Yoga

Visit a yoga studio, be sure to investigate the studio first. I went to an extremely heated (literally) yoga class with a couple of friends of mine. After about an hour of yoga at the 100 degree temperature (room was heated but maintained at the temperature) I am able to declare that I was completely anxiety free.

Float Tank

I am a big lover of total sensory loss. It's like a blend of chiropractic adjustments and massage and yoga, resulting in a surge in creativity.

A float tank is the best item that nobody is talking about or using. It's a massive tank of water at the body's temperature filled with 1,000 tonnes of Epsom salts, allowing you to can float! It's completely black and silent. After an hour of floating you can't hear you see nothing, hear nothing and you feel nothing. There is a complete absence of sensory stimulation! Imagine taking advantage of all the benefits that you'd get from an adjustment, massage or yoga at once.

Counselor/Hypnotist

It can be a wonderful opportunity to share your concerns or get someone to work with you in determining the root of your anxiety.

What supplements are you able to take to reduce stress?

* Relora

* Lemon Balm

* Kava

* Valerian Root

* St. John's Wort

* GABA

* Magnesium, a fantastic CNS (central nervous system) relaxer

There are numerous other solutions available and I would suggest several of them. I would also strongly encourage you to find the root of the problem instead of just fighting the symptoms.

Which are the top 5 tips to manage stress?

Speak to an instructor

My parents. Sometimes, I've thought of having conversations between Anthony Robbins, Brian Tracy and Napoleon Hill and asking them what they would do?

I first learned about this from the book written by Napoleon Hill called Think and Grow Rich However, I was instructed to try it in a meeting with an professional hypnotist. His books Hill discusses having meeting sessions with "ideal coaches" by asking them questions and thinking about the way they'd respond. My aim was to become more successful, motivated and free of anxiety. In this period I took part in a discussion in which I imagined my own "counselors getting together." This was a blast. The session was recorded, and I'm able to listen to it any point. After I'm done (it is only 35 minutes) I am not only I relaxed however, I am also more assured and I have an increased sense of purpose and creativeness.

Pause!

Sometimes, you need to get away. One of my most favorite activities when I'm in need of a break is to not do anything. Literally! I disconnect from the world outside. No phone, no Internet, no TV! I attempt to get out and walk my dog, or visit my parents' house in which case I'll go towards the woods, set the fire, and then relax. My two favorite activities that fall into this category include massages and floating tanks.

LAUGH!

It could be a good idea to go along with taking a break but nothing soothes the soul as much as a great comedy. Recently, I took my friends and family to an evening of Bill Burr set. It was a great time to laugh for a while. was so healing. In that light I'm on Netflix and at any time I want to relax and not be "serious," I just go to the comedy channel relax, and then laugh!

Exercise.

You are an organismand and you're designed to be a whole! You cannot have the best brain without having the best body. I do weight lifting every week, about 3 times; I also practice intervals of cardio. I workout for no more than 5 hours per week.

Deep Breathing

Many people slump and/or breathe very slowly. Oxygen is important and not just for our bodies, but to your brain! One of the most simple breathing techniques that you could try are the 1:4:2 method I mentioned earlier. Robbins recommends doing this 10 times, 3 times a week. You can also meditate using a gadget known as the emWave 2 or yoga.